Edited by Kilian McDonnell, osb

# OPEN THE WINDOWS

## The Popes
## and
## Charismatic Renewal

GREENLAWN PRESS
South Bend, Indiana

The translation of the excerpt from the encyclical *On Evangelization* is that of the United States Catholic Conference. Some use has been made of translations by the staff of *New Covenant* and the International Catholic Charismatic Renewal Office in Vatican City. The principal translator has been Rudolph Baumberger, osb.

ISBN: 0-937779-06-7

Library of Congress Catalog Card Number: 88-083044

Greenlawn Press
107 South Greenlawn
South Bend, IN 46617

© 1989 by Kilian McDonnell, osb (introductory essay) and Greenlawn Press. All rights reserved.

Printed in the United States of America
Second Printing

# CONTENTS

# PREFACE

This small collection of papal documents is modeled on *Los Papas y la Renovacion* (Bogotá: *Centro Carismático Minuto de Dios,* 1987) edited by Diego Jaramillo. The collection is not identical, and is not just a translation of Jaramillo's pamphlet, but it has borrowed from it. The translation of the documents is basically that of Rudolph Baumberger, osb. Some use was made of a translation made by the International Catholic Charismatic Renewal Office (ICCRO) in Vatican City.

Rightly or wrongly, the charismatic renewal has understood itself as one of the effects (not the only one) of Pope John XXIII's throwing open the windows to let the strong breath of God renew the church. This self-understanding seems to have been accepted by Pope Paul VI and Pope John Paul II. For this reason this small collection of documents has been entitled *Open the Windows: The Popes and Charismatic Renewal.*

As seen from my introductory essay, "Charismatic Renewal: On the Periphery or at the Center?," the collection is presented as an outreach of the ministry of ICCRO. This office sees its function as promoting the baptism in the Holy Spirit. The pamphlet is not meant to be a scholarly presentation, but is popular in intent.

The view of the baptism in the Spirit expressed in the introductory essay is my own. The basic insight into the relation between baptism in the Spirit and Christian initiation has been the common property of most theologians in the renewal from the early days. I refer also to the support which a theologian the stature of Edward Schillebeeckx gives for understanding the rites of initiation (which, for him, include the reception of the prophetic charisms) as

v

the baptism in the Holy Spirit. He is writing neither specifically of nor to the charismatic renewal, but from the theological perspective of ministry. Schillebeeckx repeatedly returns to Christian initiation as the baptism in the Holy Spirit in *The Church With a Human Face*.[1]

Each document is introduced by two sections. First, I give the date and circumstances of the document. Second, I give the main lines of the document and indicate passages of special significance. Third, I give the papal text.

For the most part, these papal addresses should not be judged as one would judge a more formal document, e.g., an encyclical. The addresses given here are more casual, sometimes more personal, more immediately pastoral, than other papal modes of expression. Care must be taken that the documents are not over-interpreted, namely, that one not read into the papal graciousness more than what a pope might say to any number of groups. The pope meets with a wide variety of conferences, congresses, associations (Catholic, Protestant, Jewish, nonreligious), and with leaders of Eastern religions. Among the Catholic groups which request audiences there are movements which also rightly understand themselves as initiatives of the Holy Spirit, where the charisms are also to be found. To each, according to its special character, the pope addresses words of encouragement and support, as well as cautions.

Even keeping in mind the nature of such papal statements, they express a remarkable witness to the papal discernment, built in part on the discernment of episcopal conferences around the world, that the charismatic renewal is one of the things that the Spirit is saying to the churches. It is to be encouraged and pastored.

Not all the documents contained in this collection refer specifically to the charismatic renewal. Some are from texts directed to the church as a whole, e.g., Pope John's prayer in preparation for the opening of Vatican II, which asks for "a new Pentecost," or Pope Paul's encyclical *On Evangelization*. These are included because they have a special impact on the charismatic renewal.

The temptation should be avoided of thinking that every

reference to the Spirit in papal documents is directed to the charismatic renewal. Nonetheless, more general papal pronouncements directed to the church at large take into account the new situation, the greater awareness of the Spirit and charisms, to which the charismatic renewal and other renewal movements have contributed. It is unlikely that the pope was not also thinking of this large international charismatic movement when writing on the Spirit. Therefore, extracts from documents addressed to the whole church have been included.

A document of a more private nature has been included in the collection, the letter of Pope Paul VI to Cardinal Suenens. It is given here not because of its theological weight, but because the popes had entrusted the pastoral care of the charismatic renewal to Cardinal Suenens. By its inclusion I wish to acknowledge the indebtedness of the renewal at the international level to Cardinal Suenens for the courage he demonstrated in supporting the renewal in the early days before it had won broad acceptance in the church, and for the guidance he still gives.

I wish to thank Colleen Thielman and Brenda Levinski for their help in preparing the manuscript, and Daniel De-Celles and Tom Noe of Greenlawn Press for locating original Italian texts and guiding the manuscript through to publication.

# CHARISMATIC RENEWAL:
# ON THE PERIPHERY OR AT THE CENTER?

Kilian McDonnell, osb

The popes have received representatives of the charismatic renewal on various occasions and spoken with them both formally and informally. However, the popes have not addressed the question of the centrality of the renewal to the life of the church, nor the centrality of the baptism in the Holy Spirit, much less the nature of the baptism. They have spoken of the importance and significance of the renewal. The task here is to link what the popes have said about the renewal to the central reality, the baptism in the Spirit.

The exposition is in three parts. First, I want to indicate the ways in which the popes expressed these convictions. Second, I wish to demonstrate how the weight and significance indicated by the popes are expressed in the renewal by the baptism in the Holy Spirit. In particular, I want to show that the baptism in the Holy Spirit is as central as the rites of Christian initiation (Baptism, Confirmation, Eucharist), of which it is an integral part. Third, in this context I want to indicate how wisely the International Catholic Charismatic Renewal Office in Vatican City has chosen as its special task the promotion of what is central to the life of the church by focusing its ministry on the baptism in the Holy Spirit.

The interpretation of the baptism in the Spirit given here is my own, but it is based on the view which from the beginning of the renewal won the widest acceptance.

At the beginning of the charismatic renewal Pope Paul VI acknowledged that reports had been received from a number of countries of new encounters with the Spirit, raising new questions about the relationship of spontaneous charismatic groups to the church. Generic references to renewal in the church by the popes made in general audiences should not be understood as applying only to the charismatic renewal. There are, of course, a number of renewal movements in the church, all prompted by the Spirit. The charisms are not limited to the charismatic renewal. Still, Pope Paul VI surely included the charismatic renewal when he acknowledged the presence of the Spirit in this new awareness of the Spirit, quoting the apostolic demand for openness, "Do not quench the Spirit" (1 Th. 5:19).[2]

The "sense of the church" will lead to the realization that charism and institution belong inseparably together. As has been said, neither Paul VI nor John Paul II has spoken directly about the nature of the baptism in the Holy Spirit, but both have mentioned the sacrament of Baptism in relation to the spiritual reality of the renewal. Paul VI, in commenting on the taste for prayer, the delight in reading the Scriptures, the effectiveness of reconciliation, pointed to the rites of initiation as their source.[3] John Paul II pointed to the joy and the dynamic as coming from the grace of Baptism.[4]

### A Perpetual Pentecost

Twice Pope Paul said that the miracle of Pentecost should continue in history.[5] The charismatic renewal is a new expression of an old reality. John Paul II reminded participants of the Sixth International Leaders' Conference in 1987 that "the history of the church is at the same time the history of two thousand years of the action of the Holy Spirit."[6] The church is part of that broad history of the Spirit. The Spirit is always doing a new thing.

The church is capable of rejuvenation because at no moment has it withdrawn from that history of the Spirit. In the new forms of life, new styles of community, the church gives evidence of that new youthfulness which is rooted in the perpetual Pentecost by which the church lives.[7] Integral to that ongoing, ever-present Pentecost are the charisms, all of which "are to be received with gratitude."[8] This is a reference to the *Dogmatic Constitution on the Church*, 12. Far from being reluctant to receive the charisms, the prayer should be that "the Lord increase even more this outpouring of charisms to make the church more fruitful."[9] While the charisms are present in the charismatic renewal, they belong, in the first instance, to the entire church, and cannot be sequestered by any groups within the church as their property.[10]

### A Certain Lived Experience

What typifies the charismatic renewal and other expressions of revitalization is "an intense spiritual quest" manifested in a rediscovery of prayer, a new love of contemplation.[11] The reappropriation of prayer and contemplation does not arise simply out of some doctrinal conviction, not simply out of "a teaching received by faith," that is, out of a knowledge of the doctrine handed on in the church; it has its source also "in a certain lived experience."[12]

The experience of God's presence impels to praise. All of this is not focused exclusively on the Spirit. To experience the Spirit is to experience Christ.[13] The renewal, then, is not a cult of the Spirit in contrast to a cult of Christ. In the experience of the Spirit Christ stands at the center in a move back to the source, the Father. Even more than this, to experience the Spirit is to be led back through Christ to the Father. The life of the renewal is caught up into the rhythm of trinitarian life.

The Spirit who draws to contemplation and praise also impels to evangelization, as a river must go beyond its source.[14] The impulse to proclaim the effective reign of God means that the risen Christ and the sent Spirit are not restricted in the plan of salvation to those who now seek God in an intense spiritual life. After Easter and Pentecost, the new reality, the new humanity, the first fruits, the pledge of a future, point to a transformed humankind in a transformed universe. The transformation has already begun, but has not yet reached its fullness. Redemption is cosmic.[15]

### Justice and Mary

If the vision is cosmic, it must be in solidarity with human goals: the dignity of persons, the poor in their call for justice. Mary in her Magnificat shows her awareness that the God who saves "cannot be separated from the manifestation of his preferential love for the poor and humble."[16] The pope has taken over the vocabulary of liberation theology to confront the renewal with the call for social justice.

Both Pope Paul VI and John Paul II return to Mary's role in the Christian life. In these repeated allusions to Mary the popes are being faithful to the living experience of the church. The Marian accent also reflects the actuality of the charismatic renewal at the international level, though the Marian content differs from country to country.

### The Privileged Generation

In any broad movement including large numbers of persons from every walk in life with everyone an active participator, there are bound to be problem areas. With great delicacy both Paul VI and John Paul II have reflected on this side of the renewal. Yet the emphasis is not on dangers, but on the opportunity which the renewal presents, a favored moment to be met with joy and gratitude. Paul VI, speaking to a conference of leaders, remarked that this was a privileged generation. "This generation can shout to the world the glory and greatness of the God of Pentecost."[17] The same pope called the charismatic renewal "a chance for the church and the world."[18] This is an opportunity which is not to be passed over. What a waste, Paul VI said, if we do not take all the means to see that this chance remains a real possibility to be exploited to the full.[19]

Paul VI returned to the same theme in a broader context when addressing the whole church (and thus not exclusively the charismatic renewal): "We live in the church at a privileged moment of the Spirit."[20]

Some years later John Paul II picked up Paul VI's reference to the privileged generation, and applied it to the charismatic renewal.[21] Neither pope is suggesting that this generation marks the first appearance of a love of prayer or a zeal for evangelization. Neither is saying that the charisms are present in the renewal for the first time in the history of the church. Neither is saying that the renewal in the church is limited to one movement. Both are saying that God is always doing a new thing. God has always done a new thing by raising up saints endowed with power, holiness and charisms. Now, in this generation, God is again doing a new thing in a new context, with new modalities, which makes this generation privileged in a new way.

Pope John Paul II described the role of the priest in the renewal as "unique and indispensable."[22] John Paul has encouraged priests to be open to the renewal, to respond positively to requests for sacramental ministry, to maintain the renewal within the mainstream of the church's life.[23] The priest cannot minister to the renewal "unless he adopts a welcoming attitude towards it."[24] To the bishops the pope said: "Your role is to encourage the renewal."[25]

When John Paul II said, "I am convinced that this movement is a sign of his (the Spirit's) action,"[26] or when he described the charismatic renewal as "an eloquent manifestation . . . a bold statement of what the Spirit is saying to the churches,"[27] he was not addressing a movement which concerns itself with peripheral aspects of the gospel.

*Baptism in the Holy Spirit as Integral to Christian Initiation*
When the International Catholic Charismatic Renewal Office asks itself how to foster the strengths to which the popes made reference, the answer is "to promote the baptism in the Holy Spirit." Though there have been various ways of explaining the baptism in the Holy Spirit, the dominant theology—and this from the beginning—has been to see baptism in the Holy Spirit in relation to the rites of initiation (Baptism, Confirmation, Eucharist).[28]

At least a probability exists that when the New Testament texts refer to baptism "they mean something ritually larger and increasingly more complex than the water bath alone."[29] The whole complex of the rites of Christian initiation corresponds *as a pattern* to the Old Testament initiation of priests.[30] So, to speak of baptism, and yet mean the whole baptismal pattern (water bath, anointing, meal), corresponds to a pattern which was already very old when taken over from the Old Testament into the New. Even before Paul the water bath, and therefore the whole complex of initiatory rites, was very likely perceived as baptism in the Holy Spirit.[31] Edward Schillebeeckx returns frequently to this expanded notion of baptism in the Holy Spirit as basic to the understanding of what the church is and what the church does.[32] He maintains that the baptism in the Holy Spirit, which is Christian initiation, was accompanied by pneumatic prophetic manifestations.[33] The spread of the church and the formation of new Christian communities, together with a web of mutually supporting ministries, were based on the baptism in the Holy Spirit and on the charisms there manifested. As Schillebeeckx specifies when speaking of ministry in biblical times, "all who received Christian baptism formed the one prophetic and pneumatic people of God."[34] Later, when ministry in the church began to have a more structured and hierarchical form, baptism in the Holy Spirit remained "the matrix of ministry."[35]

In some of the early authors in the postbiblical development, the phrase "baptism in the Holy Spirit" was still placed in relation to water baptism. Such usage can be found, for instance, in Justin Martyr (c. 100–c. 165)[36] and Didymus the Blind (c. 313-398).[37] Water baptism did not stand in isolation, but was itself part of a larger complex of initiatory rites, which included what we have come to recognize as Confirmation and also the Eucharist.

*A Second-Century Example of Baptism in the Holy Spirit*
One can see this in the case of Tertullian (c. 160–c. 225). Tertullian does not use the phrase "baptism in the Holy Spirit" but in his treatise *On Baptism*, written between 198 and 200, he described the rite of initiation as he knew it in the

church of North Africa. It consisted of a water bath, anointing, laying on of hands, and the celebration of the Eucharist.

Without suggesting that all churches in North Africa were architecturally the same, there were places where there was a separate baptistry. In the baptistry there was often a large circular pit filled with water, so that, if an adult stood in it, the water would reach to about the waist. The baptistry stood in close proximity to a larger building in which there was an altar around which the Eucharist was celebrated.

After the immersion of the candidates for baptism there was both an anointing and a laying on of hands. In his treatise *On Baptism*, Tertullian described the purpose of the imposition of hands as "inviting and welcoming the Holy Spirit."[38] At the very end of this treatise Tertullian exhorted the candidates: "Therefore, you blessed ones, for whom the grace of God is waiting, you who are about to come up from the most sacred bath of the new birth, for the first time you are spreading out your hands in your mother's house. With your brethren ask your Father, ask your Lord for a special gift of his patrimony, the abundance of charisms. Ask, he says, and you shall receive. In fact, you have sought, and you have found: you have knocked, and it has been opened to you."[39] I thank Dr. Cecil M. Robeck, Jr., who called my attention to this passage.

The sequence of events as Tertullian knew them from the church in North Africa needs to be noted. Tertullian called attention to the moment when the candidates for baptism came up from the pit of water in the baptistry where they had been immersed ("you who are about to come up from the most sacred bath of the new birth"). When the candidates ascended out of the water they lifted up and spread out their hands in a gesture of prayer ("you who for the first time spread out your hands in your mother's house"). Standing with arms outstretched and palms open was the customary posture when the community was engaged in praise. The phrase "in your mother's house" is a reference to the church, both as a physical place and as the mystery of God's grace.

It is essential to keep in mind that the candidates were moving from the water bath, the anointing and the imposition of hands to the eucharistic part of the rite of initiation. The action took place within the context of the local church, sisters and brothers gathered around the bishop for the celebration of the Eucharist. After the water bath, anointing and imposition of hands, when gathering in the larger building for the celebration of the Eucharist, Tertullian offered some pastoral advice. He suggested that the candidates ask the Father, and then the Lord Jesus Christ, for the charisms. Here Tertullian uses the more technical word *charisma* instead of the more general word *donum* (gift). Ostensibly these were the charisms which one expected to find in any normal, healthy, local communion. The charisms were the special part of the Christian inheritance.

The request for the charisms was made with the expectation that the petitioners would receive what they requested: "Ask, he says, and you shall receive." Finally Tertullian suggested that the prayer for the charisms had in fact been granted, and that the candidates had received the charisms they had asked for: "So now, you have sought, and have found: you have knocked, and it has been opened to you." The most obvious sense of the words would indicate that, for at least some of the candidates, there were some observable phenomena, which would lead others to conclude that the prayer for the charisms had been granted.

### Innovation or an Old Tradition?

Was Tertullian introducing an element here which was new and foreign? The answer is no. Tertullian, it seems, was reflecting the common experience of the church in North Africa. During the second and third centuries the presence and exercise of the charisms, including prophecy and tongues, were accepted facts of church life.

The *Didache* still understands the prophets as exercising

a function of importance in the church. Sections of the *Didache* are believed to predate the later books of the New Testament.[40] Justin Martyr (c. 100-c. 165) bragged to the Jew Trypho "that the prophetic gifts remain with us," having been taken from the Jews and given to the Christians.[41] Irenaeus (c. 130-c. 200) wrote of "the prophetic charisms," including tongues, as present in the church of his days.[42] Irenaeus was not going to allow the abuse of the gifts to pass as an excuse for abandoning the use. There are some, he said, who use the presence of false prophets as a pretext "for expelling the grace of prophecy" from the church.[43]

Tertullian did not write in order to describe how initiation might be carried out, or how he would prefer to have it celebrated. Rather, he was describing how the church of North Africa actually celebrated Christian initiation. Tertullian was a traditionalist and therefore not one given to experimentation and innovation. He held on to the old ways, to how the church had celebrated Christian initiation according to the honored tradition. In addition, liturgy, itself, is generally conservative and resists changes. Therefore Tertullian was describing a baptismal practice which already had some antiquity.

The prayer for charisms as attested in Tertullian's treatise *On Baptism*, written in the years 198-200, reflects the church of his age. His treatise is a reliable source of Catholic baptismal practice in North Africa at the end of the second century.

After he wrote *On Baptism* Tertullian became associated with the Montanists. Still, a patristic scholar the stature of Johannes Quasten has said that *On Baptism* is "free of every trace of Montanism."[44] The ancient rite described by Tertullian has the elements of what 20th-century Christians call the baptism in the Holy Spirit: laying on of hands, a petition to the Spirit to come upon the candidates, the prayer that the charisms would be given, the expectation that the charisms would be manifest at that time, evidence that the charisms had as a matter of fact been imparted. That this liturgy was the rite of initiation of new members usually celebrated at Easter or Pentecost means that it was not a secondary matter, much less peripheral, but was central to the life of the church.[45]

*Cyril: Christian Initiation = Baptism in the Holy Spirit*

A hundred and fifty years after Tertullian there is another witness to baptism in the Spirit being integral to the rites of initiation (that is, Baptism, what we today identify as Confirmation, and Eucharist). Cyril of Jerusalem (c. 315-386) has left 24 sermons, which have been called "one of the most precious treasures of Christian antiquity."[46] In about 350 Cyril preached these sermons in the newly constructed Church of the Holy Sepulcher in Jerusalem. Cyril called the rites of initiation "the baptism in the Holy Spirit."[47] His teaching on the baptism in the Spirit is based on the Scriptures and on the experience of the church of his day.[48] He witnesses to the presence of the charisms in the Christians of his diocese, in the province of Palestine, and in the whole Roman Empire.[49]

Cyril mentioned both prophecy and tongues, but he invested more interest in the former.[50] Nonetheless he recognized a wide spectrum of charisms of the Spirit: wisdom, giving alms to the needy, self-control, mercy, patience in persecution, fasting and mortification, chosen poverty, chastity, exorcism, healing, turning away from wealth and honor.[51]

Charisms are not adornments of individual Christians, but given to specific persons as members of the church. As Cyril expressed it, "(the church) possesses charisms of every kind."[52] Toward the end of the long Lenten series of instructions, and just before the celebration of Easter, Cyril told the candidates for Baptism who were about to become members of the church: "(the Spirit) will grant you charisms of every kind."[53] Therefore the charisms are in the church and of the church. For Cyril the coming of the Spirit and the imparting of the charisms at Pentecost are "the new wine, the grace of the New Testament."[54] Before, during and after the account of Pentecost, Cyril referred to the event as the moment when the apostles were "completely baptized."[55] In bringing to a close the series of 19 instructions Cyril's "final words" to the baptismal candidates were: "prepare your souls for the reception of the heavenly charisms (*charismata*)."[56]

*The New Reality*

Cyril reflected on the rites of initiation twice: before Easter, in preparing candidates for initiation during the Vigil on Holy Saturday, and after Easter, on reflecting with them on the meaning of the rites, which were then past. In this process Cyril referred to elements which are normally involved in what we today call baptism in the Holy Spirit. As we have seen, for Cyril the rites of initiation are also the baptism in the Holy Spirit.

The first element is the expectation that the charisms will be given in the rite of initiation, which has just been pointed out.

The second element is the anointing, which in the East played a larger role than the imposition of hands, but had the same function, namely, the imparting of the Spirit. For Cyril and the East this is done by the anointing along with the liturgical prayer, rather than by an imposition of hands, as was done in the West.

The third element is the coming of the Holy Spirit as related to this anointing. St. Peter said that "God anointed Jesus of Nazareth with the Holy Spirit" (Acts 10:38), a text Cyril refers to.[57] Because Jesus was anointed not with material oil, but with the Spirit, the candidates likewise are anointed all over their bodies as a symbol of the anointing with the Holy Spirit. By this anointing the candidates became "partakers and sharers of Christ."[58] Cyril, and with him the whole of antiquity, firmly believed that these rites were effective; they accomplished what they symbolized, namely, the imparting of the Spirit (and the charisms). The charisms belong to the normal functioning of the Christian community. Together with the imparted Spirit they constitute "the new reality."[59]

### Hilary: The River of God and Intense Joy

Hilary of Poitiers (c. 315-367) was a contemporary of Cyril, though we have no evidence that they knew each other or each other's works.[60] For Tertullian it was a different matter. Hilary was acquainted with Tertullian's writings, which, in fact, seem to have been readily accessible in Hilary's native Gaul. No agreement has been reached on how extensive Tertullian's influence on Hilary was, but the fact of the dependence seems assured. Though we have no direct evidence that Hilary knew Tertullian's *On Baptism*, it is not unlikely that he did. Hilary had studied both Latin and Greek. His knowledge of Greek made considerably easier the exile into which he was sent by the Emperor Constantius. For four years he remained exiled in Phrygia in Asia Minor, but he was given considerable freedom to move about, to meet Eastern bishops, and to become acquainted with their liturgical traditions. His exile was terminated in 360. He brought home with him an intimate knowledge of Greek thought and ways. Again, we have no evidence that he knew the liturgical traditions of Cyril's Jerusalem. On his return to Gaul he wrote a *Tract on the Psalms* about 364. In this work we find the text on initiation. Commenting on Psalm 64 (65) Hilary identified the Holy Spirit with the river of God which flows out from within one who believes in Jesus. Extending the image of the river of God, Hilary wrote: "From that fountain of life the water of God's river is generously poured out on us."[61] When the Spirit comes, the gifts follow: "We are inundated with the gifts (*muneribus*) of the Spirit."[62]

Within this context Hilary introduced the celebration of Christian initiation. "We who have been reborn through the sacrament of baptism experience intense joy (*maximum gaudium*), when we feel the first stirrings (*initia sentimus*) of the Holy Spirit. We begin to have insight into the mysteries of faith, we are able to prophesy and to speak with wisdom. We become steadfast in hope and receive the gift of healing. Demons are made subject to our authority. These gifts enter us like a gentle rain, and once having done so, little by little, bring forth fruit in abundance. When this gentle rain falls, the earth rejoices. But the rains are multiplied so that [at first] there are small streams: the streams [then] are filled [literally "become drunk"] so that they become rivers."[63]

We need to pay attention to the language and images Hilary used. The Spirit is not only the river of God, but a river which floods the land. When that flood inundates the candidates for Baptism they experience a profound joy. In addition, Hilary stated that these first movements of the Spirit within the believer at Baptism were a matter of experience. The experiential dimension to which Hilary pointed needs to be accepted, but it should not be pressed.

The gifts are enumerated: knowledge, prophecy, wisdom, healing and exorcism. We need not suppose that Hilary was giving a complete list of all the gifts found in the Christian community.

The gifts come in the manner of a gentle rain: softly, quietly. Hilary noted that there was a progression. At first the rain of gifts was like a small shower, so that the runoff from it formed small streams. Then the number of showers increases and the small streams, when united, become rivers. "We are inundated with the gifts of the Spirit."[64] That this rich endowment includes the charisms is evident from Hilary's citation of 1 Corinthians 12.

In his commentary on this particular psalm Hilary mentioned Baptism in the framework of the church's official morning and evening prayer, and, beyond that, in relation to the Eucharist.[65] Hilary said that one drinks from the river of God, which is the Spirit. God not only gives us drink; food is also provided. "[First] through the communion in the body of Christ (Eucharist), then in the communion of the assembled body of Christ (church), we are prepared for the company of God."[66] Through insertion into the church, the charisms are bestowed. The charisms are bestowed here because they are ministries of the church, to the church.[67]

Hilary was describing the experience of the church. We know from a random remark that Hilary was baptized as an adult. In using the language of experience to describe

Baptism, Hilary was very likely also reflecting on the experience of the church and on his own personal baptismal experience as an adult.

In the texts of Tertullian we read of specific gestures and acts; this makes it possible to identify elements which are associated with the baptism in the Spirit. Hilary was not concerned to speak about the liturgy of Baptism, but about the theological content of initiation. Therefore he says nothing about laying on of hands, or an explicit prayer for the imparting of the Spirit, or other ritual elements, which were undoubtedly part of his liturgy. Hilary does express the interior elements of baptism in the Spirit: the Spirit, as the river of God, being imparted at Baptism and flooding the land; the deep interior experience which is sometimes associated with baptism in the Spirit; the imparting of the charisms as a gentle rain.

### What Is the Central Reality?

We now have three witnesses from the early church to the baptism in the Holy Spirit, Tertullian from the end of the second century (198), Cyril and Hilary from the middle of the fourth century (350 and 364). Though the three belong to different geographical and cultural traditions, they witness together that the baptism in the Holy Spirit is one with Christian initiation. Tertullian came from the Latin West, and Cyril from the Syriac/Greek East, and Hilary, linking both traditions, was acquainted with both West and East. These three are not minor personalities. Tertullian is a major theologian, quite apart from his association with Montanism. The other two carry special weight because each has been declared Doctor of the church, Cyril by Pope Leo XIII, and Hilary by Pope Pius IX.

However, a presentation such as I have just given has its dangers. The impression might be given that the rites of initiation as the baptism in the Holy Spirit are simply the instruments for obtaining charisms. This would be a major distortion.

The rites of initiation are the introduction into the Body of Christ, the sacraments by which one enters into and participates in the mysteries of Christ's death and resurrection, thus becoming a part of a worshipping, evangelizing community. The charisms are not the central reality. They are by-products. In the days of Cyril, for instance, it would have been considered, at the very least, exceedingly strange to seek what he calls the baptism in the Spirit *in order to* receive a charism. That would indicate that the seeker has not understood the prebaptismal instructions.

On the contrary, because one has become a participator in the mystery of the death and resurrection of Jesus, and tasted his Body and Blood, and become a member of the church, one is given a ministry/charism. The purpose of the charism is to promote the life of the community and of humankind, and thereby to be of benefit to the individual.

Another danger is that of routinization and formalism. These dangers are present in all the sacraments. That is, sometimes the sacraments are approached in a mechanical way, with little subjective preparation, little awareness of their real significance. Besides the objective nature of the sacraments as acts of Christ, there is a subjective element. If one receives the sacraments in a routine, careless way, or without an attempt to know what they signify, all of this affects the fruitfulness of the sacrament. God usually (not necessarily) takes us where we are.

The charisms represent a broad spectrum of ministries. The lists in Paul (Rom. 12:6-8; 1 Cor. 12:28-30; Eph. 4:11) do not seem to be exhaustive. At least in Luke tongues and prophecy have a privileged relationship to baptism in the Spirit (Acts 2:1-4; 10:44-48; 19:1-6).

Care should be taken not to consider charisms as commodities or as spiritual objects. Charisms are the way the power of the Holy Spirit comes to "visibility" in a ministry to church and world.

If one finds such clear evidence for charisms in the rites of initiation in Tertullian, Cyril and Hilary, why did the charisms not persist in the tradition? The answer has to do with the reaction to the excesses of Montanism, a charismatic movement arising in the second half of the first century. The logic went like this: the Montanists championed the charisms; Montanism was thought by many to be a heresy; therefore charisms themselves became suspect.

### Private Piety or Public Liturgy?

Specific elements which are associated with baptism in the Holy Spirit as understood in the charismatic renewal today are present in the ancient rites of Christian initiation as seen in Tertullian, Cyril and Hilary. This would indicate that baptism in the Holy Spirit does not belong to private piety but to public, official, corporate liturgy of the church. What the charismatic renewal today understands as baptism in the Holy Spirit is an integral part of the initiation of all Christians. If all of this is true, one cannot look upon baptism in the Holy Spirit as a pious practice, or a matter of purely private devotion.

This places baptism in the Holy Spirit in a wholly new light. Baptism in the Holy Spirit is not special grace for some, but common grace for all. Baptism in the Holy Spirit is integral to those sacraments (Baptism, Confirmation, Eucharist) which are constitutive of the deepest nature of the church. In a real sense these sacraments make the church. All attempts to say what the church is, what the sources of the church's life are, have their origin here. The reality of the baptism in the Holy Spirit belongs to that primary spiritual reality which makes the church to be church.[68]

### Integral Conversion

No claim is made that the baptism in the Holy Spirit is captive to the charismatic renewal. On the contrary, the claim is that, because it is integral to initiation, it belongs to the life of the whole church. Neither is a claim made that the reality of which the baptism in the Holy Spirit is an expression can be found only in prayer groups or covenant communities. The forms in which it can be given expression are as varied as the forms of community in the church. Nor does the baptism in the Holy Spirit, and what flows from it, belong to the theologically conservative as over against the theologically liberal. Least of all is there a claim that the dynamic of the baptism in the Spirit is limited to purely interior renewal.

In Christian initiation the word of God is proclaimed and the mysteries of Christ are celebrated. From the days of Pope Pius X the liturgy has been recognized as the "primary and indispensable source of the true Christian spirit." The true Christian spirit is still wanting where the joy of which Hilary spoke is entirely lacking, a joy which issues again in the hunger for God, in adoration, in praise. A measure of contemplation is part of the Christian vocation. If baptism in the Spirit is integral to initiation then it is also the source which all evangelization takes as its point of departure. The proclamation that Jesus is Lord starts here.

The orientation toward evangelization is essential. To insist on the charisms is not to suggest that they be highlighted, as though they should dominate Christian consciousness. Though a quiet prophet would be something of an anomaly, all charisms need not be front, center and noisy. The operative word is "normal." A church preoccupied with charisms would have small claim to be embodying the norm. The charisms are rather a premise to the day to day life of the normal healthy communion. They are suppositions implicit within the communion, as the church engages in the task of proclaiming the Lordship of Jesus and the gospel demand for peace and justice. The preoccupation of the renewal is not with charisms, but with the hunger for God and evangelization.

If baptism in the Spirit is integral to Christian initiation, then it is also part of that paradigm for social transformation which demands liberation and justice for the poor, dignity and equality for women, a living wage for those who labor, sharing of talents and resources of wealthy nations with developing countries. The whole vast program for social justice and social transformation finds its source and strength there where the word of God is proclaimed and the mysteries of Christ are celebrated in the liturgy, in Christian initiation.

The goal of the charismatic renewal is integral renewal,

integral conversion, in which the interior transformation is made visible outwardly in social patterns and institutions. An inward conversion without outward conversion is an untruth. There must be no privatized, overspiritualized, foreshortened, truncated vision of what God wants for the church and world. One cannot choose between interior conversion and social justice; one must choose them both. A purely interior renewal is too timid for the God of Pentecost.

### The Ministry of ICCRO: To Promote the Baptism in the Holy Spirit

The charismatic renewal is therefore not concerned with peripheral, secondary or tertiary matters. However imperfectly the charismatic renewal actualizes these ideals in the church, the reality to which the renewal points is that reality which is at the center of the church's life. The renewal has its life from the church, in the church.

The dominant theological understanding of the baptism in the Holy Spirit—and this from the beginning of the Catholic charismatic renewal—is based on the rites of initiation. The renewal is as central to the life of the church as the rites of initiation. The experience of baptism in the Spirit today is, then, a reappropriation, a new experience and awareness, of the graces given at initiation. How this is done at various levels of the church's life (parishes and nonparochial communities) demands great pastoral wisdom and sensitivity. When ICCRO took as its special concern to promote the baptism in the Holy Spirit, it was, in effect, ensuring that all the strengths mentioned by the popes would be rooted in the life of the church, not alongside it. The hunger for God, the deep contemplative prayer, the love of praise, the rediscovery of community, the view of the community as wholly ministerial (everybody in the church has a ministry), solidarity with the poor (in some countries), the inescapable imperative to evangelize —all flow from the power of the Spirit imparted at the center of what makes the church.

The great emphasis on evangelization in the international renewal is also an expression of the missionary character of Christian life which has its base in those initiatory sacraments which are constitutive of the church. Therefore ICCRO has wanted to promote evangelization by defining its own ministry as that of promoting the baptism in the Holy Spirit.

## PRAYER FOR THE COUNCIL 1961

*On December 25, 1961, Pope John XXIII formally convoked Vatican Council II to meet the following year. At the end of the apostolic constitution convoking the council the pope called to mind the scene of the apostles gathered in Jerusalem after the Ascension, waiting for the promised Spirit. To this description the pope added a prayer for "a new Pentecost."*

What happened at Pentecost is the model for what should happen in the entire Christian people, including churches separated from Rome. The communion of thought and prayer in the newborn church is a communion with and around Peter. When Pope John XXIII published his prayer for the council it was prophetic of a number of renewal movements in the church, among them the charismatic renewal. What the pope asked for was nothing less than renewal of the wonders of the first Pentecost.

## GIVE US A SECOND PENTECOST

May there be repeated thus in Christian families the spectacle of the apostles gathered together in Jerusalem after the Ascension of Jesus to heaven, when the newborn church was completely united in communion of thought and of prayer with Peter and around Peter, the shepherd of the lambs and of the sheep. And may the Divine Spirit deign to answer in a most comforting manner the prayer that rises daily to him from every corner of the earth.
. . . Renew your wonders in our time, as though for a new Pentecost, and grant that the holy church, preserving unanimous and continuous prayer, together with Mary the Mother of Jesus, and also under the guidance of St. Peter, may increase the reign of the Divine Savior, the reign of truth and justice, the reign of love and peace. Amen.

## THE ANNOUNCEMENT
## OF THE HOLY YEAR 1973

*On Pentecost, 1973, Pope Paul VI called the church to celebrate a Holy Year, first throughout the world and then in Rome.*

*With a startling image the pope asks us to get downwind of the Spirit, so that we will not miss what the Spirit is doing in scarcely perceptible ways. To be noted is the impulse, the dynamic, moving all believers in the direction of the fulfillment of the new age which began at the time of the Paschal Mystery, that is, Easter and Pentecost. Though now already caught up in that movement toward complete realization, it has not yet reached that perfect fulfillment when the goal of history will have been reached, and God will be all in all. In a special way this is the work of the Spirit.*

## GET DOWNWIND OF THE SPIRIT

All of us need to place ourselves downwind from the breath of the Holy Spirit, the mysterious breath which even now cannot be completely defined. The fact that the Holy Year unfurls its sails in the individual local churches precisely on this blessed day of Pentecost is not without significance. This date has been chosen in the hope that all believers may be carried in a single direction, and in harmony with one another, striving toward the new goal of Christian history, its eschatological port.

## FIRST INTERNATIONAL LEADERS' CONFERENCE 1973

*The participants in the First International Leaders' Conference at Grottaferrata, October 8-12, 1973, numbered 120 delegates from 34 countries, among them two bishops. The conference considered such themes as communications and unity, mature leadership, preparation for baptism in the Holy Spirit, and the unity of the renewal at the national level in each country. A document was written, whose publication was approved by the Congregation for the Doctrine of the Faith.[69] Participants in the congress also attended the pope's general audience on October 10, 1973. After the general audience 13 of the leaders in the renewal met with the pope in a brief private audience. The pope greeted each leader and spoke to them in French.*

*It seems evident that at this date Rome is still in a discernment process with regard to the renewal. During the general audience no mention was made of the renewal. At this stage the more common names such as "renewal in the Spirit," "community renewal," "charismatic renewal" were not employed by the pope. During the private audience his careful language was more generic. Pope Paul VI referred to the movement as one concerned with the renewal of the spiritual life. Though at this stage there is a reluctance to identify the renewal too specifically, the pope accurately describes its most typical expressions: persons are drawn to deep prayer and contemplation, a focus on praise, generosity in ministries, a love of the Scriptures, and a commitment to one another. In all these the pope discerns the work of the Spirit. The omission of any reference to the charisms is to be noted, a sign not of disapproval but of the still tentative judgment the pope wishes to maintain.*

*The pope emphasizes the relation of the individual groups to the local church, the bishop of which has the special task of discernment. The task of discernment is to identify the authentic from the spurious. Nonetheless, the accent is on the need not to extinguish the Spirit. All gifts are ordered to the common good of*

*the church. The appearance in the church of such groups arouses*
*many hopes for the renewal of the whole church.*

*The pope refers this renewal movement to chapter 12 of the*
Dogmatic Constitution on the Church (Lumen Gentium),
*which has to do with the prophetic office of Jesus and the char-*
*isms in the Christian life. This section declares that the Holy*
*Spirit "distributes special graces among the faithful of every*
*rank," and that the charisms "are to be received with thanksgiv-*
*ing and consolation for they are exceedingly suitable and useful*
*for the needs of the church." In the charismatic renewal the pope*
*recognizes the reality of which the council wrote.*

*The very last paragraph contains comments which the pope*
*informally added to his prepared text.*

## DISCERN BUT DO NOT EXTINGUISH
## THE SPIRIT

We rejoice with you, dear friends, at the renewal of the
spiritual life manifested in the church today, in different
forms and in various environments. Certain common notes
appear in this renewal: the taste for deep prayer, personal
and in groups, a return to contemplation and an emphasis
on praise of God, the desire to devote oneself completely
to Christ, a great availability for the calls of the Holy Spirit,
more assiduous reading of the Scriptures, generous broth-
erly devotion, the will to make a contribution to the service
of the church. In all that, we can recognize the mysterious
and discreet work of the Spirit, who is the soul of the
church.

The spiritual life consists above all in the exercise of the
virtues of faith, hope and charity. It finds its foundation in
the profession of faith. The latter has been entrusted to the
pastors of the church to keep it intact and help it to de-
velop in all the activities of the Christian community. The
spiritual lives of the faithful, therefore, come under the active pastoral responsibility of each bishop in his own diocese. It is particularly opportune to recall this in the presence of these ferments of renewal which arouse so many
hopes.

Even in the best experiences of renewal, moreover,

weeds may be found among the good seed. So the work of discernment is indispensable; it devolves upon those who are in charge of the church, those "to whose special competence it belongs, not indeed to extinguish the Spirit, but to test all things and hold fast to that which is good (cf. 1 Th. 5:12,19-21)" (*Lumen Gentium*, 12). In this way the common good of the church, to which the gifts of the Spirit are ordained, is fostered (cf. 1 Cor. 12:7).

We will pray for you that you may be filled with the fullness of the Spirit and live in the Spirit's joy and holiness. We ask for your prayers and we will remember you at Mass.

Document 4

## THE SYNOD OF BISHOPS 1974

*On October 10, 1974, when the synod of bishops was being celebrated in Rome, Pope Paul VI referred to the charismatic renewal. A book by Cardinal Suenens entitled* A New Pentecost? *had just appeared. The pope mentioned it explicitly, and completed the written text he was carrying with an extended improvisation, recorded and broadcast by Vatican Radio.*

*The pope stresses the relation of the Spirit to the love which is imparted to us by the redemptive work of Christ in the Holy Spirit. There is a trinitarian dynamic at work: the Father sends the Son to effect the redemption, and the Spirit to sanctify and to provide access in the Spirit through the Son back to the Father. The Spirit, while dwelling in the church, does a work of communion. To the Spirit is ascribed the work of making new again, returning the church to the vigor of the church's youth. Through the Spirit the church experiences the wonder of a perpetual Pentecost.*

*For the first time in a public, as contrasted with a private, address, the pope speaks explicitly of charisms. Somewhat in the manner of the renewal in France, the pope speaks of the baptism in the Spirit as "the effusion of charisms." The charisms are multiple and are ministries. These charisms which were abundant in the early church seem to have been given "more economically" later, a reference to the general absence of some of the prophetic charisms. Still, in every age God has raised up saints who possessed wondrous charisms. The pope prays for a more abundant rain of charisms, which makes the church more fruitful. The charisms make the church capable of demanding respect, arousing the attention and wonder of the profane world. The prayer for an outpouring of the charisms is directed specifically to the work of evangelization.*

*The pope mentions the book by Cardinal Suenens, which speaks of the reasons why the church might expect a major outpouring of charisms.*

*The Spirit is not controlled, but comes to dwell where there is expectancy, listening, humility. The mention of expectancy is especially important in the pope's remarks, indicating that openness to the charisms has some role to play in their being present. God usually—not necessarily but usually—takes us from wherever we are. If there is not openness to the charisms, usually they will not be present.*

*Like Mary and the apostles we must know how to wait and call for the Spirit. Today the church needs all that the Spirit brings.*

*These remarks of Pope Paul VI are the most forceful he had addressed to the renewal up to this point.*

## THE VITAL BREATH OF GRACE

The church lives by the infusion of the Holy Spirit: infusion, which we call grace, that is, the gift *par excellence*, charity, love of the Father communicated to us in the Holy Spirit by virtue of the redemption fulfilled by Christ. Let us remember the synthesis of Saint Augustine: "What the soul is in the body of man, this the Holy Spirit is to the Body of Christ, which is the church."

I will speak of a well-known truth. All of us have heard it repeated and proclaimed by the recent council: "When the work which the Father had given to the Son to do on earth (cf. Jn.17:14) was accomplished, the Holy Spirit was sent on the day of Pentecost in order that he might forever sanctify the church, and thus all believers would have access to the Father through Christ in the one Spirit (cf. Eph. 2:18). He is the Spirit of life . . . . The Spirit dwells in the church and in the hearts of the faithful as in a temple (cf. 1 Cor. 3:16; 6:19). In them he prays and bears witness to the fact that they are adopted sons (cf. Gal. 4:6; Rom. 8:15-16, 26). The Spirit guides the church into the fullness of truth (cf. Jn. 16:13) and gives her a unity of fellowship and service. He furnishes and directs her with various gifts, both hierarchical and charismatic, and adorns her with the fruits of his grace (cf. Eph. 4:11-12; 1 Cor. 12:4; Gal. 5:22). By the power of the gospel he makes the church grow, perpetually renews her . . . " (*Lumen Gentium*, 4).

### A New Pentecost

We must repeat, grace is required, that is, a divine intervention surpassing the natural order, both to accomplish our personal salvation and to fulfill God's redemptive plan for the whole church and all humanity, whom the mercy of God is calling to salvation . . . . This absolute need for grace presumes an essential lack on the part of man, the need for the marvel of Pentecost to continue, in the history of the church and of the world, in the twofold form in which the gift of the Holy Spirit is granted to men. First, to sanctify them. This is the primary and indispensable form. By it man is converted into the object of God's love.

But now I would say that our curiosity—yet it is a very legitimate and beautiful curiosity—is focussed on another aspect. When the Holy Spirit comes, he grants gifts. We already know of the seven gifts of the Holy Spirit, but he also gives other gifts which are today called, . . . well, now . . . , they have always been called, charisms. What is the meaning of "charism"? It means "gift." It means a grace. They are particular graces given to one person for another, in order to do good. One receives the charism of wisdom in order to become a teacher, and another receives the gift of miracles in order to perform deeds which, through wonder and admiration, call others to the faith, etc.

These kinds of charismatic gifts are gratuitous gifts — obviously not necessary, of course — but are given out of the superabundant economy of the Lord. The Lord wishes to make the church richer, more animated and more capable of defining herself, of documenting herself, and this is precisely called "the effusion of charisms." Today much is said about it. Having taken into account the complexity and delicateness of the subject, we cannot but desire that these gifts come — and may God grant it — with abundance. Besides grace, let God's church also be able to obtain and possess the charisms.

### The Rain of Charisms

The saints, that is to say, the Fathers, especially Saint Ambrose and Saint John Chrysostom, have said that charisms were abundant in former times. The Lord gave this great, may we call it, "rain of gifts" to animate the church, to make her grow, to strengthen her, to support her. Later, the economy of these gifts has been, I would say, more discreet, more . . . economic. Yet always there have been saints who have worked wonders. Exceptional men have always existed in the church. God grant that the Lord would still increase this rain of charisms to make the church fruitful, beautiful, marvelous and capable of inspiring respect, even the attention and the amazement of the profane world, the secular world.

We will mention a book that has been written recently by Cardinal Suenens, entitled *A New Pentecost?* He describes and justifies this expectation, which can really be something historically providential in the church, that is, the great expectation for a greater outpouring of supernatural graces, which are called charisms.

Now we direct our attention to the principal conditions for the gift of God *par excellence*. This gift is precisely the Holy Spirit, whom, we know, "breathes where he wills." But he does not reject the longing of anyone who waits for him, calls on him and welcomes him (even when this long-

ing itself proceeds from one's own intimate inspiration).
What are these conditions? Let us simplify a difficult answer by saying that the ability to receive this "sweet guest
of the soul" exacts faith. It demands humility and repen-
tance. Normally, it requires a sacramental act. In the practice of a religious life, it requires silence, recollection, listening and, above all, invocation, prayer, as the apostles
did with Mary in the Cenacle. It is important to wait and
to cry out: "Come, Creator Spirit; come, Holy Spirit."

If the church knows how to dispose herself for the new
and perennial coming of the Holy Spirit, he, the "Light of
hearts," will not delay in giving himself, for joy, light, for-
titude, apostolic virtue and unitive charity, all of which the
church has need of today.

Thus may it be. With our apostolic blessing.

Document 5

## SECOND INTERNATIONAL
## LEADERS' CONFERENCE 1975

*To celebrate the Holy Year members of the charismatic renewal
met in Rome in a general international conference from May 16 to
19, 1975. Ten thousand pilgrims celebrated the theme of "The
Renewal and Reconciliation." Two cardinals and 10 bishops accompanied them. During the previous days, May 12 to 15, the
Second International Leaders' Conference took place.*

*At noon on May 19, Pope Paul VI entered Saint Peter's Basili-
ca amid a storm of flashes from thousands of cameras and jubilant
songs of "alleluia" and praise. The pope spoke in four languages:
French, English, Spanish and Italian. Translations are given in
the order they were spoken.*

*Pope Paul VI points to the ecclesial nature of the renewal. The
desire of the leaders to see the renewal not as "a movement in the
church, but as the church itself in movement," as Heribert Müh-*

len has phrased it, is a sure sign of its authenticity. The first Pentecost did not occur outside the church, but in the midst of the church gathered with Mary in expectant prayer. The theme of Mary and Pentecost will be one which will occupy the renewal. Pope John Paul II never ended an address to a charismatic group without a word about Mary.

By its nature the event of Pentecost is a perpetual one. Pentecost is always present wherever the church is present. The need for a perpetual Pentecost today is great. Even orthodox believers, who worship the true Lord of the heavens, think and act as though the human person is its own end, as though the personal history of each believer is entirely the doing of that person alone.

In describing the renewal the pope mentions specifically the deeply personal nature of this prayer in the lives of individuals and in prayer groups. Such prayer is fed not just by an objective faith, what some might call extrinsic faith. Here the pope recognizes the personal moment in faith. The prayer to which the pope refers arises "in a certain lived experience." The experiential is a dimension of faith. A special quality of the experience is the inevitability with which it leads to praise. Beyond this it means being in right relation to God. Those who search for God are not motivated by the desire for conquest. No, they seek to respond to the love which first moved toward them.

How could such a renewal fail to be " 'a chance' for the church and for the world"? Opportunities of this kind must not be allowed to slip away. This is a strong statement, indicating that the church should be aware of this favored moment and not let it go unexploited.

If the charismatic renewal is the church in movement rather than a movement in the church, then the spiritual gifts which are manifested need to be honored and discerned, especially by those to whom such a ministry has been entrusted. The pope sets forth three principles for discernment found in the letters of St. Paul.

1. True charisms are in accord with authentic doctrine.

2. All spiritual gifts are to be received with gratitude. The pope wants the true prophetic gifts found in the church to be welcomed. This would include such gifts as prophecy and tongues. The lists of the gifts found in Paul's writings are not exhaustive.

*Authentic gifts are given not for the good of the individual re-*
*ceiving them, but for the the common good, for the community.*
*The pope indicates that there is a hierarchy of gifts. "Hierarchy"*
*suggests the image of a ladder, on which some gifts are placed*
*higher than others. Every authentic gift does not serve the com-*
*mon good to the same degree. The relatively high or low place on*
*the hierarchy or ladder is determined by the immediacy with*
*which the charism serves the common good. Those serving the*
*common good more directly are placed higher than those serving*
*the common good less directly.*

*3. No endowment with charisms by itself makes one pleasing*
*to God. Love alone does that. The Spirit introduces the believer*
*into the flow of love by which the Father loves the Son in the*
*Holy Spirit. Because the Spirit places us in that mutuality and*
*reciprocity of trinitarian love, we ourselves love God with this*
*same divine love. Here the pope returns to a trinitarian dynamic*
*or movement, not just to a static threeness. He focuses on the*
*trinitarian dynamic, namely, the mutual flow of love and life*
*which is proper to the Father reaching through the Son in the*
*Spirit to touch and transform the church and world, and to lead*
*all back through the Son in the Spirit to the Father. However*
*wondrous and necessary the charismatic gifts, love is of a more*
*primary order.*

*In his comments in English the pope again notes how the*
*renewal develops "a taste for prayer," a delight in reading the*
*Scriptures, and reconciliation. All these graces flow from the rites*
*of initiation (Baptism, Confirmation and Eucharist).*

*Protestations of love are not enough when the poor among us*
*suffer. Those who are in pain and deprivation ask for demonstra-*
*tions of love which result in making available to them the word of*
*God, both spiritual and bodily food, and a life with dignity, life*
*on a human scale.*

*In his comments in Italian the pope expresses his wish that*
*Christians would experience the joy of the Spirit. What a privi-*
*leged generation! This generation can "shout out to the world the*
*glory and the greatness of the God of Pentecost." The "drinking"*
*the Spirit which has been so generously poured out should be*
*characterized by both joy and sobriety.*

# THE AUTHENTIC SIGN

You have chosen the city of Rome in this Holy Year to celebrate your third international conference, dear sons and
daughters. You have asked us to meet you today and to
address you: you have wished thereby to show your at-
tachment to the church founded by Jesus Christ and to
everything that this See of Peter represents for you. This
strong desire to situate yourselves in the church is an
authentic sign of the action of the Holy Spirit. For God became man in Jesus Christ, of whom the church is the Mystical Body; and it is in the church that the Spirit of Christ
was communicated on the day of Pentecost when he came
down upon the apostles gathered in the upper room, "in
continuous prayer," with Mary, the mother of Jesus (see
Acts 1:13,14).

### The History of the Spirit

As we said last October in the presence of some of you,
the church and the world need more than ever that "the
miracle of Pentecost should continue in history" (*L'Osserva-
tore Romano*, October 17, 1974). In fact, inebriated by his
own conquests, modern man has finished by imagining,
according to the expression used by the last council, that
he is free "to be an end unto himself, the sole artisan and
creator of his own history" (*Pastoral Constitution on the
Church in the Modern World (Gaudium et Spes)*, 20). Alas!
Among how many of those very people, who continue by
tradition to profess God's existence and through duty to
render him worship, God has become a stranger in their
lives.

Nothing is more necessary to this more and more secu-
larized world than the witness of this "spiritual renewal"
that we see the Holy Spirit evoking in the most diverse
regions and milieux. The manifestations of this renewal are
varied: in a profound communion of souls, in intimate
contact with God, in fidelity to the commitments under-
taken at Baptism, in prayer—frequently in group prayer, in
which each person, giving personal expression freely, aids,
sustains and fosters the prayer of the others—and, at the

root of everything, a personal conviction, which does not have its source solely in a teaching received by faith, but also in a certain lived experience. This lived experience shows that without God man can do nothing, that with him, on the other hand, everything becomes possible: hence this need to praise God, thank him, celebrate the marvels that he works everywhere about us and within us. Human existence rediscovers its "relationship to God," what is called "the vertical dimension," without which one is irremediably crippled. Not, of course, that this "search for God" appears as a desire for conquest or possession; it wishes to be a pure acceptance of him who loves us and gives himself freely to us, desiring, because he loves us, to communicate to us a life that we have to receive freely from him, but not without a humble fidelity on our part. This fidelity must know how to unite action to faith according to the teaching of St. James: "For as the body apart from the spirit is dead, so faith apart from works is dead" (Jas. 2:26).

*The Renewal as a Chance for the Church and the World*

How then could this "spiritual renewal" not be "a chance" for the church and for the world? And how, in this case, could one not take all the means to ensure that it remains so?

These means, dear sons and daughters, the Holy Spirit will certainly wish to show you himself, according to the wisdom of those whom the Holy Spirit himself has established "as guardians, to feed the church of God" (Acts 20: 28). For it is the Holy Spirit who inspired St. Paul with certain very precise directives, directives that we shall content ourself with recalling to you. To be faithful to them will be for you the best guarantee for the future.

You know the great importance that the apostle attributed to "the spiritual gifts." "Do not quench the Spirit," he wrote to the Thessalonians (1 Th. 5:19), while immediately adding, "test everything, hold fast what is good" (v. 21). Thus he considered that discernment was always necessary, and he entrusted the task of testing to those whom he had placed over the community (see v. 12). With the Corinthians, a few years later, he enters into great detail: in particular, he indicates to them three principles in the light of which they will more easily be able to practice this indispensable discernment.

*St. Paul's Teaching on Charisms*

1. The first principle by which he begins his presentation is fidelity to the authentic doctrine of the faith (1 Cor. 12:1-3). Anything that contradicted it would not come from the Spirit: he who distributes his gifts is the same one who inspired the Scriptures and who assists the living magisterium of the church, to whom, according to the Catholic faith, Christ entrusted the authentic interpretation of these Scriptures. This is why you experience the need for an ever deeper doctrinal formation: biblical, spiritual and theological. Only a formation such as this, whose authenticity must be guaranteed by the hierarchy, will preserve you from ever-possible deviations and give you the certitude and joy of having served the cause of the gospel without "beating the air" (1 Cor. 9:26).

2. The second principle: all spiritual gifts are to be received with gratitude; and you know that the list is long (1 Cor. 12:4-10; 28-30), and does not claim to be complete (cf. Rom. 12:6-8; Eph. 6:11). Given, nevertheless, "for the common good" (1 Cor. 12:7), they do not all procure this common good to the same degree. Thus, the Corinthians are to "desire the higher gifts" (v. 31), those most useful for the community (see 14:1-5).

3. The third principle is the most important one in the thought of the apostle. This principle has suggested to him one of the most beautiful pages, without a doubt, in all literature, to which a recent translator has given an evocative title: "Above all hovers love" (E. Osty). No matter how desirable spiritual goods are—and they are desirable— only the love of charity, *agape*, makes the Christian perfect; it alone makes people pleasing to God. This love not only presupposes a gift of the Spirit; it implies the active presence of his person in the heart of the Christian. The Fa-

thers of the church commented on these verses, vying
with one another to explain them. In the words of Saint
Fulgentius, to quote just one example: "The Holy Spirit
can give every kind of gift without being present himself;
on the other hand, he proves that he is present by grace
when he gives love" (*Contra Fabianum*, Fragment 28: PL
65:791). Present in the soul, he communicates to it, with
grace, the most blessed Trinity's own life, the very love
with which the Father loves the Son in the Holy Spirit (Jn.
17:26), the love by which Christ has loved us and by which
we, in our turn, can and must love our brethren, that is,
"not in word or speech but in deed and in truth" (1 Jn.
3:18).

### Love Is of a More Primary Order

The tree is judged by its fruits, and St. Paul tells us that
"the fruit of the Spirit is love" (Gal. 5:22)—love such as he
has just described in his hymn to love. It is to love that are
ordered all the gifts which the Spirit distributes to whom
he wills, for it is love which builds up (see 1 Cor. 8:1), just
as it is love which, after Pentecost, made the first Christians into a community dedicated to fellowship (see Acts 2:
42), everyone being "of one heart and soul" (Acts 4:32).

Be faithful to the directives of the great apostle. Also, in
accordance with the teaching of the same apostle, be faithful to the frequent and worthy celebration of the Eucharist
(see 1 Cor. 11:27-29). This is the way that the Lord has chosen in order that we may have his life in us (see Jn. 6:53).
In the same way approach with confidence the sacrament
of Reconciliation. These sacraments express the fact that
grace comes to us from God, through the necessary media-
tion of the church.

Beloved sons and daughters, with the help of the Lord,
strong in the intercession of Mary, Mother of the Church,
and in communion of faith, of charity and of the apostolate
with your pastors, you will be sure of not deceiving yourselves. Thus you will contribute, for your part, to the renewal of the church. Jesus is Lord! Alleluia!

*Renewal and Ecclesial Communion*

*[The following is the Spanish summary spoken by the pope.]*

On the occasion of your third international conference you have desired to come here to demonstrate your adherence to the church and to the Chair of Peter. This desire to insert yourself into the church is an authentic sign of the action of the Spirit, who works in her, the Mystical Body of Christ.

All spiritual renewal necessary to the church and the world today has to come from that solid base of ecclesial communion, which is a communion of spirit and purpose in absolute fidelity to the doctrine of the faith. From this flows the search for the means necessary to make God present in people's minds. This presence has to be nourished by an increasing cultivation of supernatural values, by an intimate contact with God and by prayer. All of this enables one to transcend the human and to place it in a true perspective before God and others. Collaborate in this way to build up the church.

*Renewal and Reconciliation*

*[The following is the English summary spoken by the pope.]*

We are happy to greet you, dear sons and daughters, in the affection of Christ Jesus, and in his name to offer you a word of encouragement and exhortation for your Christian lives.

You have gathered here in Rome under the sign of the Holy Year. You are striving in union with the whole church for renewal—spiritual renewal, authentic renewal, Catholic renewal, renewal in the Holy Spirit. We are pleased to see signs of this renewal: a taste for prayer, contemplation, praising God, attentiveness to the grace of the Holy Spirit, and more assiduous reading of the sacred Scriptures. We know likewise that you wish to open your hearts to reconciliation with God and other human beings.

For all of us this renewal and reconciliation are a further development of the grace of divine adoption, the grace of our sacramental Baptism "into Christ Jesus" and "into his

16

death" (Rm. 6:3), in order that we "might walk in newness of life" (v. 4).

Always give great importance to this sacrament of Baptism and to the demands that it imposes. St. Paul is quite clear: "You must consider yourselves dead to sin but alive to God in Christ Jesus" (v. 11). This is the immense challenge of genuine sacramental Christian living, in which we must be nourished by the Body and Blood of Christ, renewed by the sacrament of Reconciliation, sustained by the grace of Confirmation and refreshed by humble and persevering prayer. This is likewise the challenge of opening your hearts to your brethren in need. There are no limits to the challenge of love: the poor and the needy and afflicted and suffering across the world and near at hand all cry out to you, as brothers and sisters of Christ, asking for the proof of your love, asking for the word of God, asking for bread, asking for life. They ask to see a reflection of Christ's own sacrificial, self-giving love—love for his Father and love for his brethren.

Yes, dear sons and daughters, this is the will of Jesus: that the world should see your good works, the goodness of your acts, the proof of your Christian lives, and glorify the Father who is in heaven (see Mt. 5:16). This indeed is spiritual renewal and only through the Holy Spirit can it be accomplished. This is why we do not cease to exhort you earnestly "to desire the higher gifts" (1 Cor. 12:31). This was our thought yesterday, when on the Solemnity of Pentecost we said: "Yes, this is a day of joy, but also a day of resolve and determination: to open ourselves to the Holy Spirit, to remove what is opposed to his action, and to proclaim, in the Christian authenticity of our lives, that Jesus is Lord."

*Shout to the World the Glory of the God of Pentecost*
*[At this point the pope's official text ends and his informal address in Italian begins.]*

Very dear ones: It is permissible to add a few words in Italian [applause], in fact, two messages. One is for those of you who are here with the charismatic pilgrimage. The other is for those pilgrims who are present by chance at this great assembly.

First, for you: reflect on the two-part name by which you are designated, "Spiritual Renewal." Where the Spirit is concerned we are immediately alert, immediately happy to welcome the coming of the Holy Spirit. More than that, we invite him, we pray to him, we desire nothing more than that Christians, believing people, should experience an awareness, a worship, a greater joy through the Spirit of God among us. Have we forgotten the Holy Spirit? Certainly not! We want him, we honor him and we love him, and we invoke him. You, with your devotion and fervor, you wish to live in the Spirit. [applause] This [applause] . . . and this should be where the second part of your name comes in—a renewal. It ought to rejuvenate the world, give it back a spirituality, a soul, religious thought. It ought to reopen its closed lips to prayer and open its mouth to song, to joy, to hymns and to witnessing. It will be very fortuitous for our times, for our brothers, that there should be a generation, your generation of young people, who shout out to the world the glory and the greatness of the God of Pentecost. [applause] In the hymn, in the hymn which we read this morning in the breviary, and which dates back as far as St. Ambrose in the third or fourth century, there is this phrase which is so hard to translate, yet should be very simple: *Laeti*, which means "joyfully," *bibamus*, "let us drink," *sobriam*, that means "well-defined and well-moderated," *profusionem spiritus* "the outpouring of the Spirit." *Laeti bibamus sobriam profusionem spiritus*. This could be a formula indicating your program.

The second message is for those pilgrims present at this great assembly who do not belong to your movement. They should unite themselves with you to celebrate the feast of Pentecost—the spiritual renewal of the world, of our society and of our souls—so that they, too, devout pilgrims to this center of the Catholic faith, might nourish themselves on the enthusiasm and the spiritual energy

with which we must live our religion. We will say only
this: today, either one lives one's faith with devotion,
depth, energy and joy, or that faith will die out.


Document 6


EXHORTATION *ON EVANGELIZATION* 1975

*On December 8, 1975, in the apostolic exhortation* On Evangelization in the Modern World (Evangelii Nuntiandi), *Pope
Paul VI collected the themes and discussions of the third general
assembly of the synod of bishops which had been held the previous year. Though obviously not directed specifically to the charismatic renewal, the encyclical teaches on areas of concern to it,
and for this reason is included here. The excerpt is limited to section 75.*

*Following in the tradition of the early Fathers of the church,
the pope points out the great theological significance of Jesus' own
baptism at the Jordan. At this moment the Father sends the Spirit on Jesus to identify who Jesus is, and to empower him for mission. When Jesus is sent out on his mission he is baptized in the
Spirit. Then the Spirit leads him into his hour of trial in the desert. When he begins preaching, Jesus announces: "The Spirit of
the Lord is upon me." In imitation of his own mission from the
Father, Jesus breathes the Spirit on his disciples before sending
them out on their missions.*

*As Jesus' baptism in the Spirit is at the beginning of his public
life, so Pentecost, the baptism in the Spirit for the apostles, is the
beginning of the evangelization of the world by the infant church.
Paul, too, is filled with the Spirit before he becomes the Apostle
of the Gentiles. The Spirit is given to those who proclaim the
word, as well as to those who hear it. What was true of the
church in its beginning is true also today. If there is no Spirit
present, there is no evangelization.*

*Of course, we need to study the techniques of evangelization,
but techniques will be the empty sound of a timbrel, an empty*

*gesture, without the Spirit. The power to evangelize is the power of the Spirit.*

*We live in a privileged moment in the life of the church. We are recapturing the biblical teaching on the Spirit. What is discovered is that the Spirit is "the principal agent of evangelization." More than that, the Spirit is the goal. Through the Spirit humanity lives in newness of life. Through the Spirit one reads the signs of the times, the signs which God has erected to mark out our way.*

*Pastors, theologians and the faithful need to study the nature and form of the action of the Spirit in evangelization.*

## EVANGELIZATION AND PENTECOST

Evangelization will never be possible without the action of the Holy Spirit. The Spirit descends on Jesus of Nazareth at the moment of his baptism when the voice of the Father—"This is my beloved Son with whom I am well pleased" (Mt. 3:17)—manifests in an external way the election of Jesus and his mission. Jesus is "led by the Spirit" to experience in the desert the decisive combat and the supreme test before beginning this mission (Mt. 4:1). It is "in the power of the Spirit" (Lk. 4:41) that he returns to Galilee and begins his preaching at Nazareth, applying to himself the passage of Isaiah: "The Spirit of the Lord is upon me." He proclaims: "Today this Scripture has been fulfilled" (Lk. 4:18,21; cf. Is. 61:1). To the disciples whom he was about to send forth he says, breathing on them: "Receive the Holy Spirit" (Jn. 20:22).

In fact, it is only after the coming of the Holy Spirit on the day of Pentecost that the Apostles depart to all the ends of the earth in order to begin the great work of the church's evangelization. Peter explains this event as the fulfillment of the prophecy of Joel: "I will pour out my Spirit" (Acts 2:17). Peter is filled with the Holy Spirit so that he can speak to the people about Jesus, the Son of God (cf. Acts 4:8). Paul too is filled with the Holy Spirit (Acts 9:17) before dedicating himself to his apostolic ministry, as is Stephen when he is chosen for the ministry of service and later on for the witness of blood (cf. Acts 6:5,

10; 7:55). The Spirit, who causes Peter, Paul and the Twelve to speak, and who inspires the words that they are to utter, also comes down "on those who heard the word" (Acts 10:44).

It is in the "consolation of the Holy Spirit" that the church increases (Acts 9:31). The Holy Spirit is the soul of the church. It is he who explains to the faithful the deep meaning of the teaching of Jesus and of his mystery. It is the Holy Spirit who, today just as at the beginning of the church, acts in every evangelizer who allows himself to be possessed and led by him. The Holy Spirit places on his lips the words which he could not find by himself, and at the same time the Holy Spirit predisposes the soul of the hearer to be open and receptive to the Good News and to the kingdom being proclaimed.

### A Privileged Moment of the Spirit

Techniques of evangelization are good, but even the most advanced ones could not replace the gentle action of the Spirit. The most perfect preparation of the evangelizer has no effect without the Holy Spirit. Without the Holy Spirit the most convincing dialectic has no power over the heart of man. Without him the most highly developed schemas resting on a sociological or psychological basis are quickly seen to be quite valueless.

We live in the church at a privileged moment of the Spirit. Everywhere people are trying to know him better, as the Scripture reveals him. They are happy to place themselves under his inspiration. They are gathering about him; they want to let themselves be led by him. Now if the Spirit of God has a preeminent place in the whole life of the church, it is in her evangelizing mission that he is most active. It is not by chance that the great inauguration of evangelization took place on the morning of Pentecost, under the inspiration of the Spirit.

It must be said that the Holy Spirit is the principal agent of evangelization; it is he who impels each individual to proclaim the gospel, and it is he who in the depths of consciences causes the word of salvation to be accepted and understood. Yet it can equally be said that he is the goal of evangelization: he alone stirs up the new creation, the new humanity of which evangelization is to be the result, with that unity in variety which evangelization wishes to achieve within the Christian community. Through the Holy Spirit the gospel penetrates to the heart of the world, for it is he who causes people to discern the signs of the time – signs willed by God – which evangelization reveals and puts to use within history.

The bishops' synod of 1974, which insisted strongly on the place of the Holy Spirit in evangelization, also expressed the desire that pastors and theologians – and we would also say the faithful marked by the seal of the Spirit by Baptism – should study more thoroughly the nature and manner of the Holy Spirit's action in evangelization today. This is our desire, too, and we exhort all evangelizers, whomever they may be, to pray without ceasing to the Holy Spirit with faith and fervor and to let themselves prudently be guided by him as the decisive inspirer of their plans, their initiatives and their evangelizing activity.

Document 7

## LETTER TO CARDINAL SUENENS 1978

*From early in the history of the renewal Cardinal Suenens has guided it into the mainstream of the church's life. Without his discernment, the renewal would most likely not have won its comparatively quick acceptance by the church at large. His stance was a daring one. This May 27, 1978, letter of Paul VI acknowledges Cardinal Suenens's role in the process of the church's discernment and integration.*

## FULL INTEGRATION INTO THE CHURCH
To our venerable Brother Leo Josef Suenens Archbishop of Malines-Brussels: We have read with much attention the

letter which you addressed to us this past April 15 concerning the charismatic renewal movement. We could not have communicated to you as rapidly as we would have desired our pleasure at the attentive care with which you have watched over this movement in order to ensure its full integration into the life of the Catholic Church. We are happy today to tell you how much we appreciate this effort. We ask the Lord to fill you with his grace in this ecclesial service, and to you, from our heart, we renew an affectionate Apostolic Blessing.

> *The Vatican, May 27, 1978*
> *Paul VI*

Document 8

## THIRD INTERNATIONAL LEADERS' CONFERENCE 1978

*On the occasion of the Third International Leaders' Conference of the charismatic renewal, assembled in Dublin in June, 1978, Pope Paul VI sent a telegram through Jean Cardinal Villot.*

*The pope again gives public evidence of his regard for the renewal. He specifically gives thanks for the charisms with which the participants minister in the church. Wishing the participants to live at the heart of the church, he encourages them to transform their sacramental life so that they can give themselves to the great needs of the church in communion with the hierarchy and the whole church. He wishes that the outpouring of the Spirit would transform them so that they could be witnesses of Christian authenticity.*

## GIFTS AND FRUITS IN THE COMMUNION

The Holy Father sends greetings of joy and peace to those who are taking part in the international conference of charismatic renewal of the Catholic Church. He gives thanks to God for the divine gifts which presently perform their function in the lives of many sons and daughters of the Catholic Church.

His Holiness prays that the great fruits of the Holy Spirit may sustain the participants in a Christian life genuinely sacramental, leading them on to grow in a sensitive manner according to the immense needs of the whole Body of Christ, and confirming them in a total collaboration with the hierarchy and in ecclesiastic unity with the entire church.

Also, he prays that, by means of the effusion of the Holy Spirit, the evangelical testimony of all the participants may be perfect, to such a degree that they can proclaim effectively in the Christian authenticity of their daily lives that Jesus Christ is Lord.

With these sentiments, the Holy Father with pleasure sends his Apostolic Blessing.

*Jean Cardinal Villot*
*The Vatican,*
*June 18, 1978*

Document 9

## AUDIENCE WITH
## THE INTERNATIONAL COUNCIL 1979

*On December 11, 1979, Pope John Paul II received in special audience Cardinal Suenens, Bishop Alfonso Uribe, and the members of the Council of the International Office of the Charismatic Renewal. The audience, which lasted an hour and a half, began with a videotape on the renewal which had been prepared for viewing by the pope.*

*In the past the intellectual aspect of faith had a kind of dominance which excluded the affective dimension of the faith, or gave it scant attention. The charismatic renewal is also present in Poland, but it is like another edition of the same book. That is, it is less lively there.*

*The pope recalls the charismatic dimension of his own life, a prayer to the Holy Spirit given to him by his father. Faithful to this prayer to the Spirit, the pope has no difficulty understanding the variety of charisms. He sees the charismatic renewal as a sign that the Spirit is still acting in the church.*

*The charismatic movement is needed as an answer to materialism. The coming of the Spirit also leads us to our full and true humanity. The charismatic renewal is an important part of all the movements renewing the church.*

### A Revolution of the Faith

Thank you! It was an expression of faith. Indeed, the singing, the words and the gestures. It is . . . how does one say it? I can say that it is a revolution of this living expression (of the faith). We say that the faith is a matter of the intelligence, and at times also of the heart, but this expressive dimension of the faith has been absent. This dimension of the faith was diminished, indeed, inhibited, scarcely there. Now we can say that this movement is everywhere, also in my country. But it is different there. In Poland, it is not so expressive. I can say that in Poland the mentality is the same, but in another edition.

*After these words came greetings, information on the renewal, and an informal dialogue about the different aspects of the renewal. Then the pope made the following comments:*

## THE SIGN OF THE SPIRIT'S ACTION

This is my first meeting with you, Catholic charismatics. Even so, I still cannot respond to this petition (sic). First, permit me to explain my own charismatic life.

I have always belonged to this renewal in the Holy Spirit. My own experience is very interesting. When I was in school, at the age of 12 or 13, sometimes I had difficulties in my studies, in particular with mathematics. My father gave me a book on prayer. He opened it to a page and said to me: "Here you have the prayer to the Holy Spirit. You must say this prayer every day of your life." I have remained obedient to this order that my father gave nearly 50 years ago, which I believe is no little while. This was my first spiritual initiation, so I can understand all the different charisms. All of them are part of the riches of the Lord.

I am convinced that this movement is a sign of his action. The world is much in need of this action of the Holy Spirit, and it needs many instruments for this action. The situation in the world is dangerous, very dangerous. Materialism is opposed to the true dimension of human power, and there are many different kinds of materialism. Materialism is the negation of the spiritual, and this is why we need the action of the Holy Spirit. Now I see this movement, this activity everywhere. In my own country I have seen a special presence of the Holy Spirit. Through this action, the Holy Spirit comes to the human spirit, and from this moment we begin to live again, to find our very selves, to find our identity, our total humanity. Consequently, I am convinced that this movement is a very important component in the total renewal of the church, in this spiritual renewal of the church.

*[At the conclusion of the audience, there was a time dedicated to prayer. Then the pope said:]*

Pray for the peoples who cannot express themselves, for those who suffer persecution under the laws, those who cannot speak of their faith in Christ. Keep them in your hearts.

*[One year later, on writing Pope John Paul II a letter asking him if they should continue praying for the same intentions, Bishop Eduardo Martinez, Substitute Secretary of State at the Vatican, responded in the name of the pope:]*

His Holiness wishes to reaffirm his deep gratitude for the fervent support of the charismatic renewal in the whole world, and at the same time he is grateful for their promise of loyalty and solidarity in the faith. The Holy Father would be grateful if you would continue praying for the intentions that he had already made known to them, since these same remain close to his heart and are very important for the mission of the church.

## THE APOSTOLIC EXHORTATION
## *ON CATECHESIS* 1979

*An extract from the apostolic exhortation* On Catechesis (Catechesi Tradendae), *published October 16, 1979, is given here, namely, section 72.*

*To catechize is a form of evangelization. Therefore it is proper to direct attention to the role of the Spirit. To live in the church now is to live in a period when persons are more aware of the presence and action of the Spirit. If one is looking for signs of the renewal's authenticity, they are not so much to be found in the appearance in the renewal of unusual charisms—though we know from other papal statements that these too are to be received with gratitude—as by knowing and living out the full mystery of Christ.*

## A NEW CATECHETICAL DYNAMISM

It is necessary that the profound desire to understand better the action of the Spirit and to surrender oneself more to him brings about a catechetical awakening—given that "we live in the church at a privileged moment of the Spirit," as my predecessor Paul VI observed in his apostolic exhortation *Evangelii Nuntiandi.* "Renewal in the Spirit will be authentic and will have real fruitfulness in the church, not so much according as it gives rise to extraordinary charisms, but according as it leads the greatest possible number of the faithful, as they travel their daily paths, to make a humble, patient and persevering effort to know the mystery of Christ better and better and to bear witness to it."

I now invoke over the catechizing church this Spirit of the Father and of the Son, and entreat him to renew a catechetical dynamism in the church.

## FIRST AUDIENCE WITH THE ITALIAN CHARISMATIC RENEWAL 1980

*On Sunday, November 23, 1980, John Paul II received 16,000 of those involved in the Italian charismatic renewal. It was the first time since becoming pope that he had publicly addressed a group representing the charismatic renewal.*

*The Holy Father refers to the baptism in the Holy Spirit as "the effusion of the Spirit" and acknowledges that those in the renewal owe to it "a deeper and deeper experience of Christ." This is a clear statement that the baptism in the Spirit is a Christ-centered event. Every experience of the Spirit is an experience of Christ. The baptism is acknowledged as being that which was promised by the Risen Christ and actualized on the first Pentecost when the Spirit came down in power upon the assembled, witnessing to Jesus, speaking in tongues as the Spirit gave them utterance. The further history in the Acts of the Apostles presents the Spirit as active in both leaders and the faithful.*

*The Christ-centered character of this experience of the Spirit brought the early Christians to the conviction that anyone who did not have the Spirit did not belong to Christ, and therefore the Spirit is not to be grieved, the movement of the Spirit is not to be quenched, and Christians are to be led by the Spirit. The one who sows in the Spirit reaps eternal life.*

*Easter and Pentecost represent the new reality, the new creation, which is cosmic in scope: not just the renewal of the interior life, but the rebirth of all humanity, the transformation of the created universe. This has already begun, but it has not reached the fullness yet to come.*

*We who live at the end of the second millennium should see*

28

that the plan of salvation is the decisive and irrevocable commu-
nication of God in Christ, and that the actuality of the Risen
Christ in human experience is the permanent work of the Spirit.
Only in the Spirit can one acknowledge Jesus as Lord. The Spirit
it is who makes the Body of Christ one, who manifests the divine
power in a multiplicity of charisms.

Yet the Spirit also manifests the power of God as society moves
toward the fuller realization of the human goals of justice, love
and freedom.

To the individual believer the Spirit gives "special graces"
directed to the renewal of the church. All this implies risk, because the Spirit is active in fragile earthen vessels, which at times
restrict his free movement. The risks can even be identified: excessive attention to emotional experience, pursuit of the unusual,
fanciful interpretation of Scripture, preoccupation with self,
avoidance of apostolic commitment. Though these risks are present in the renewal, they are not restricted to it.

Therefore test, discern and embrace what is found to be good.
Remain available to every gift which the Spirit wishes to pour
out in abundance. Every charism is destined for the common
good. We know that love is the more primary reality, which gives
value to the charisms. Docility to the Spirit will lead to docility
toward those who have the ministry of oversight in the church.
True renewal is authentic not so much in the pursuit of extraordinary charisms, as in daily fidelity to the demands of the Christian life, and to bearing patient witness to the mystery of Christ.

The pope commends participants in the renewal to the protection of Mary who conceived through the power of the Holy Spirit. To rediscover Pentecost is to find Mary. This is not just a
theological insight, but reflects the experience of the renewal at
the international level.

## AUTHENTIC RENEWAL

Beloved Brothers and Sisters!!

Thank you, in the first place, for this joyful visit, and in
particular for the prayers you have addressed to the Lord
for me and for the responsibilities of my pastoral service. I
will say to you with St. Paul that, "I longed to see you,
that I might impart to you some spiritual gift to strengthen

you, that is, that we might be mutually encouraged by each other's faith, both yours and mine" (Rm. 1:11-12).

This morning I have the joy of meeting this assembly of yours, in which I see young people, adults, old people, men and women, united in the profession of the same faith, sustained by longing for the same hope, bound together by bonds of that charity which "has been poured into our hearts through the Holy Spirit which has been given to us" (Rm. 5:5).

To this effusion of the Spirit we know we owe a deeper and deeper experience of the presence of Christ, thanks to which we can grow daily in loving knowledge of the Father. Rightly, therefore, your movement pays particular attention to the action, mysterious but real, that the third person of the Holy Trinity plays in the Christian's life.

The words of Jesus in the Gospel are explicit: "I will pray the Father, and he will give you another Counselor, to be with you forever, even the Spirit of truth, whom the world cannot receive, because it neither sees him nor knows him; you know him, for he dwells with you, and will be in you" (Jn. 14:16-17).

Before ascending to heaven, Jesus promises the apostles again that they will be baptized "with the Holy Spirit" (Acts 1:5) and, full of his power (Acts 2:2), they will bear witness to him all over the world, speaking "in other tongues, as the Spirit gives them utterance" (Acts 2:4). In the book of Acts the Spirit is presented as active and operating in those whose deeds are told, whether they are the leaders of the community (Acts 2:14-18; 4:5-22; 5:29-32; 9:17; 15:28; etc.) or just members of the faithful (Acts 4:31-37; 10:45-47; 13:50-52; etc.).

*Completing the "New Creation"*

It is not surprising that the Christians of that time drew from these experiences the deep conviction that "anyone who does not have the Spirit of Christ does not belong to him" (Rm. 8:9), and therefore felt committed not "to quench the Spirit" (1 Th. 5:19), not to "grieve him" (Eph. 4:30), but to be led by him (Gal. 5:18), sustained by the

30

hope that "the one who sows in the Spirit will from the Spirit reap eternal life" (Gal. 6:8).

In fact, Christ entrusted to the Spirit the mission of completing the new creation, which he himself started with his resurrection. From the Spirit, therefore, must be expected the progressive regeneration of the universe and of humanity, between the "already" of the Passover and the "not yet" of the parousia.

It is important that we, too, Christians set by Providence to live in the conclusive years of this second millennium, should revive a deep awareness of the mysterious ways through which divine Providence carries out the plan of salvation. God communicated himself irrevocably in Christ. It is by means of the Spirit, however, that the Risen Christ lives and acts permanently in our midst and can make himself present in every here and now of human experience in history.

With deep joy and fervent gratitude we renew, therefore, our act of faith in Christ the redeemer, well aware that "no one can say 'Jesus is Lord' except by the Holy Spirit" (1 Cor. 12:3). It is he who united us in a single body in the unity of the Christian vocation and in the multiplicity of charisms. It is he who carries out the sanctification and unity of the church.

### Concern of Vatican Council II

The Second Vatican Council reserved special attention for the multiform action of the Spirit in the history of salvation. It stressed the "wondrous Providence" with which he drives society to evolve toward more and more advanced goals of justice, love and freedom. It illustrated his presence operating in the church, which is urged by means of an ever deeper understanding of revelation, and kept whole in the flow of time, thanks to an ever renewed commitment of sanctification and communion in charity.

The council pointed out, finally, the Holy Spirit's action in each of the faithful, whom he stimulates to a courageous apostolic testimony, strengthening them by means of the sacraments and enriching them with "special graces . . . .

By these gifts he makes them fit and ready to undertake the various tasks or offices advantageous for the renewal and building up of the church."

What wide perspectives, beloved sons and daughters, open up before our eyes! Certainly there is no lack of risks, because the action of the Spirit takes place "in earthen vessels" (2 Cor. 4:7), which may compress its free expansion.

You know what they are: excessive weight given, for example, to emotional experience of the divine; unrestrained pursuit of the spectacular and the extraordinary; tolerance of hasty and distorted interpretations of Scripture; withdrawal into one's self; shunning apostolic commitment; narcissistic gratification which isolates itself and shuts itself up. These and others are the risks that appear on your way, and not only on yours.

I will say to you with St. Paul: "Test everything; hold fast what is good" (1 Th. 5:21). Remain, therefore, in an attitude of constant and grateful availability for every gift that the Spirit wishes to pour into your hearts, never forgetting, however, that there is no charism that is not given "for the common good" (1 Cor. 12:7). Aspire, in any case, to "the higher gifts" (1 Cor. 12:31). And you know, in this connection, what appears on an even more stupendous page of Scripture: St. Paul indicates the way of love, which alone gives meaning and value to other gifts (1 Cor. 13).

### Of One Heart and Soul

Animated by love, not only will you listen spontaneously and docilely to those whom "the Holy Spirit has made overseers, to care for the church of God" (Acts 20:28), but you will also feel the need of an increasingly attentive understanding of your brothers and sisters, in the desire to come to be with them "of one heart and soul" (Acts 4:32). From this will come the real renewal of the church, which the Second Vatican Council desired and which you endeavor to stimulate with prayer, witness and service.

"Renewal in the Spirit, in fact," as I recalled in the apostolic exhortation *Catechesi Tradendae*, "will be authentic and will have real fruitfulness in the church, not so much according as it gives rise to extraordinary charisms, but according as it leads the greatest possible number of the faithful, as they travel their daily paths, to make a humble, patient and persevering effort to know the mystery of Christ better and better, and to bear witness to it" (section 72).

Invoking upon you and your commitment the loving and assiduous protection of her who "through the Holy Spirit" conceived in her womb and gave birth to the incarnate Son of God (Lk. 1:35), I willingly grant you my Apostolic Blessing, and extend it to all those who are members of the movement, and to all the persons who are dear to you in the Lord.

Document 12

## FOURTH INTERNATIONAL LEADERS' CONFERENCE 1981

*During the Fourth International Leaders' Conference, the week of May 4-10, 1981, Pope John Paul II received participants on five occasions: He gave an audience to Cardinal Suenens, had lunch with members of the International Council, celebrated the Eucharist with some priests, and invited the delegates of Poland to have supper with him. He also participated in a prayer meeting which took place in the Vatican Gardens at the Grotto of Our Lady of Lourdes, Thursday, May 7, from 8:00 to 9:30 p.m. There, the pope spoke to the 600 delegates from almost 100 countries.*

*The pope summarized the three principles of discernment of which Pope Paul VI had spoken to the Third International Conference in 1975 (See page 23). John Paul II recalled that six years previously Paul VI had spoken of the renewal as "a chance for the church and the world." That this had proven true is evidenced in the pursuit of holiness and the love of the word of God. Also the* pope noted a deeper awareness of social-justice issues, a deficiency which critics of the renewal have often remarked.

In comparison to the earlier conference six years previously, there is a greater ecclesial vision. The task of a leader is to deepen that awareness through the prayer tradition of the church inherited from the past, a living experience which comes in many forms: meditation on Scripture, openness to the gifts without concentration on the more unusual gifts, love of the sacraments and private prayer, regard for the church's liturgical life, especially the Liturgy of the Hours, the center of all prayer being the celebration of the Eucharist. This would seem to be an attempt by the pope, without disparaging new prayer forms which have emerged in the renewal, to remind leaders that there is a vast treasure of prayer forms in the living tradition of the church. These, too, arise out of experience.

Leaders need to provide solid spiritual food for others, principally the explanation of the word of God as interpreted by the church. In the Scriptures will be found the clear teaching on the dignity of the human person. The theme of such dignity has been often repeated by the pope in a variety of contexts.

Fostering trust and cooperation with the bishops is also the work of a leader. Building this confidence is the task of the leaders even when the bishop does not share the style of prayer which has enriched the renewal. In such an instance leaders need to remember that in the rite of the ordination of a bishop the prayer of the church is that the Spirit will be poured out on the ordinand so that he might wisely govern the church committed to his care. John Paul II notes the many statements on the charismatic renewal which national episcopal conferences have issued, giving encouragement and support. The pope acknowledges that these documents from national hierarchies are an important element of the work of discernment. Both the pope in his role in the universal church, and the bishops in theirs in the local church, constitute one integral process of listening and judging. Both are necessary.

Priests are cooperators in the pastoral ministry of the bishop and should have a "welcoming attitude" toward the renewal so that the renewal will not form "alternate and marginal structures," but can be integrated into the apostolic and sacramental life of the parish. Here the pope has touched on an issue with which most segments of the renewal have had to deal. If priests are not open and welcoming, it is difficult to integrate the renewal into the life of the local church.

The ecumenical dimension of the renewal was not tacked on after a considerable period of time, but emerged with the first beginnings. The ecumenical dimension has continued to be an integral expression of the renewal. The pope seems to be recognizing the importance which the renewal can play in the ecumenical task. Not the least among the spiritual realities which the renewal shares with separated brothers and sisters are the many gifts of the Spirit. This places the renewal in a position of advantage to further "the serious task of ecumenism." First in the ecumenical priorities for Catholics is the renewal of the Catholic Church. All ecumenism starts with spiritual renewal at home. The doctrinal convergence must not be sacrificed in a rush to create "a kind of autonomous church of the Spirit" separate from the visible church. This seems to be a reference to the danger of "a churchless Christianity." Such a vaporizing of the church occurs when persons ask, "If we have Jesus and the Bible, do we really need the church?"

Finally, the pope recalls that the woman called by God to cooperate in the work of salvation in a special way is Mary, who was always docile to the promptings of the Spirit.

## RESPONSIBLE LEADERSHIP

Dear brothers and sisters in Christ,

In the joy and peace of the Holy Spirit I welcome all of you who have come to Rome to participate in the Fourth International Leaders' Conference of the Catholic charismatic renewal, and I pray that "The grace of the Lord Jesus Christ, and the love of God, and the fellowship of the Holy Spirit be with you all!" (2 Cor. 13:13).

Your choice of Rome as the site of this conference is a special sign of your understanding of the importance of being rooted in that "Catholic unity of faith and charity" which finds its visible center in the See of Peter. Your reputation goes before you, like that of his beloved Philippians, which prompted the Apostle Paul to begin his letter to

them with a sentiment I am happy to echo: "I give thanks
to my God every time I think of you . . . . My prayer is
that your love may more and more abound both in understanding and wealth of experience, so that with a clear
conscience and blameless conduct you may learn to value
the things that really matter, up to the very day of Christ"
(Ph. 1:3, 9-10).

*Memories of Paul VI*

In 1975 my venerable predecessor Paul VI addressed the international charismatic conference which assembled here
in Rome, and he emphasized the "three principles" which
Saint Paul outlined "to guide discernment," according to
the injunction: "Test everything, hold fast what is good"
(1 Th. 5:21). The first of these principles is "fidelity to the
authentic doctrine of the faith"; whatever contradicts this
doctrine does not come from the Spirit. The second principle is "to value the higher gifts" — the gifts which are given
in service of the common good. The third principle is "the
pursuit of charity," which alone brings the Christian to
perfection: as the apostle says, "Over all these virtues put
on love, which binds the rest together and makes them
perfect" (Col. 3:14). It is no less important at this time for
me to underline these fundamental principles for you
whom God has called to serve as leaders in the renewal.

Pope Paul described the movement for renewal in the
Spirit as "a chance for the church and for the world," and
the six years since that conference have borne out the hope
that inspired his vision. The church has seen the fruits of
your devotion to prayer in a deepened commitment to
holiness of life and love for the word of God. We have noted with particular joy the way in which leaders of the renewal have more and more developed a broadened ecclesial vision, and have made efforts to make this vision
increasingly a reality for those who depend on them for
guidance. We have likewise seen the signs of your generosity in sharing God's gifts with the unfortunate of this
world in justice and charity, so that all people may experience the priceless dignity that is theirs in Christ. May

this work of love already begun in you be brought to successful completion! (cf. 2 Cor. 8:6, 11). In this regard, always remember these words which Paul VI addressed to your conference during the Holy Year: "There are no limits to the challenge of love: the poor and the needy and afflicted and suffering across the world and near at hand all cry out to you, as brothers and sisters of Christ, asking for the proof of your love, asking for the word of God, asking for bread, asking for life."

### An Enriched Vision of the Church

Yes, I am very happy to have this opportunity to speak from my heart to you who have come from all over the world to participate in this conference designed to assist you in fulfilling your role as leaders in the charismatic renewal.

In a special way I wish to address the need for enriching and making practical that ecclesial vision which is so essential to the renewal at this stage in its development.

The role of the leader is, in the first place, "to give the example of prayer" in his own life. With confident hope, with careful solicitude, it falls to the leader to ensure that the multiform patrimony of the church's life of prayer is known and experienced by those who seek spiritual renewal: meditation on the word of God, since "ignorance of Scripture is ignorance of Christ," as Saint Jerome insisted; openness to the gifts of the Spirit, without exaggerated concentration upon the extraordinary gifts; imitating the example of Jesus himself in ensuring time for prayer alone with God; entering more deeply into the cycle of the church's liturgical seasons, especially through the Liturgy of the Hours; the appropriate celebration of the sacraments —with very special attention to the sacrament of Reconciliation—which effect the new dispensation of grace in accord with Christ's own manifest will; and above all a love for and growing understanding of the Eucharist as the center of all Christian prayer. For, as the Second Vatican Council has impressed upon us, "The Eucharist shows itself to be the source and the apex of the whole work of preaching the gospel. Those under instruction are introduced by stages to a sharing in the Eucharist" (*Decree on the Ministry and Life of Priests (Presbyterorum Ordinis)*, 5).

Second, you must be concerned to provide solid food for spiritual nourishment through the "breaking of the bread of true doctrine." The love for the revealed word of God, written under the guidance of the Holy Spirit, is a pledge of our desire to "stand firm in the gospel" preached by the apostles. It is this same Holy Spirit, the *Dogmatic Constitution on Divine Revelation* assures us, who "constantly brings faith to completion by his gifts . . . to bring about an ever deeper understanding of revelation" (*Dei Verbum*, 5). The Holy Spirit who distributes his gifts, now in greater, now in lesser measure, is the same one who inspired the Scriptures and who assists the living magisterium of the church, to whom Christ entrusted the authentic interpretation of these Scriptures (cf. Address of Paul VI, May 19, 1975), according to the promise of Christ to the apostles: "I will ask the Father and he will give you another Paraclete, to be with you always: the Spirit of truth, whom the world cannot accept, since it neither sees him nor recognizes him, but you can recognize him because he remains with you and will be within you" (Jn. 14:16-17).

God desires, therefore, that all Christians grow in understanding the mystery of salvation, which reveals to us ever more of man's own intrinsic dignity. And he desires that you who are leaders in this renewal should be ever more deeply formed in the teaching of the church whose bimillennial task it has been to meditate on the word of God, in order to plumb its riches and to make them known to the world. Take care, then, that as leaders you seek a sound theological formation designed to ensure for you, and all who depend upon you for guidance, a mature and complete understanding of God's word: "Let the word of Christ, rich as it is, dwell in you. In wisdom made perfect, instruct and admonish one another" (Col. 3:16-17).

*Trust and Cooperation*

Third, as leaders in the renewal, you must take the initiative in building bonds of "trust and cooperation with the bishops," who have the pastoral responsibility in God's providence for shepherding the entire Body of Christ, including the charismatic renewal. Even when they do not share with you the forms of prayer which you have found so enriching, they will take to heart your desire for spiritual renewal for yourselves and for the church, and they will offer you the sure guidance which is the task allotted to them. The Lord God does not fail to be faithful to the promise of their ordination prayer, in which he was implored to "pour out upon these chosen ones that power which is from you, the governing Spirit whom you gave to your beloved Son, Jesus Christ, the Spirit given by him to the holy apostles, who founded the church in every place to be your temple for the unceasing glory and praise of your name" (Rite of Ordination of a Bishop). Many bishops throughout the world, both individually and in statements of their episcopal conferences, have given encouragement and direction to the charismatic renewal – and at times even a helpful word of caution – and have assisted the Christian community at large to understand better its place in the church. By this exercise of their pastoral responsibility, the bishops have offered a great service to us all, in order to ensure for the renewal a model of growth and development fully open to all the riches of the love of God in his church.

*Role of the Priest*

At this time I would also like to call your attention to another point of special relevance to this conference of leaders: it concerns "the role of the priest" in the charismatic renewal. Priests in the church have received the gift of ordination as cooperators in the pastoral ministry of the bishops, with whom they share one and the same priesthood and ministry of Jesus Christ, which requires their strict hierarchical communion with the order of bishops (*Presbyterorum Ordinis*, 7). As a result the priest has a unique and indispensable role to play in and for the charismatic renewal as well as for the whole Christian community. His mission is not in opposition to or parallel to the legitimate role of the laity. Through the priest's sacramental bond with the bishop, whose ordination confers a pastoral responsibility for the whole church, he helps to ensure for movements of spiritual renewal and lay apostolate their integration with the sacramental, liturgical life of the church, especially through participation in the Eucharist; there we say, "Grant that we, who are nourished by his body and blood, may be filled with his Holy Spirit, and become one body, one spirit in Christ" (Third Eucharistic Prayer). The priest shares in the bishop's own responsibility for preaching the gospel, for which his theological formation should equip him in a special way. As a result, he has a unique and indispensable role in guaranteeing that integration with the life of the church which avoids the tendency to form alternative and marginal structures, and which leads to a fuller sharing, especially in the parish, in her sacramental and apostolic life. The priest, for his part, cannot exercise his service on behalf of the renewal unless and until he adopts a welcoming attitude toward it, based on the desire he shares with every Christian by Baptism to grow in the gifts of the Holy Spirit.

You leaders of the renewal, then, priests and laity, must witness to the common bond that is yours in Christ, and set the pattern for that effective collaboration which has for its charter the Apostle's injunction: "Make every effort to preserve the unity which has the Spirit as its origin and peace as its binding force. There is but one body and one Spirit, just as there is but one hope given all of you by your call" (Eph. 4:3-5).

### Task of Ecumenism
Finally, by your experience of many gifts of the Holy Spirit which are shared also with our separated brothers and sisters, yours is the special joy of growing in a desire for the unity to which the Spirit guides us and in a commitment to "the serious task of ecumenism."

40

How is this task to be carried out? The Second Vatican Council instructs us: "the Catholic's primary duty is to make a careful and honest appraisal of whatever needs to be renewed and done in the Catholic household itself, in order that its life may bear witness more loyally and luminously to the teachings and ordinances which have been handed down from Christ through the apostles" (*Decree on Ecumenism (Unitatis Redintegratio)*, 4). Genuine ecumenical effort does not seek to evade the difficult tasks, such as doctrinal convergence, by rushing to create a kind of autonomous "church of the Spirit" apart from the visible church of Christ. True ecumenism, rather, serves to increase our longing for the ecclesial unity of all Christians in one faith, so that "the world may be converted to the gospel and so be saved, to the glory of God" (*Unitatis Redintegratio*, 1). Let us be confident that, if we surrender ourselves to the work of genuine renewal in the Spirit, this same Holy Spirit will bring to light the strategy for ecumenism which will bring to reality our hope of "one Lord, one faith, one baptism, one God and Father of all, who is over all, and works through all, and is in all" (Eph. 4:6).

Dear brothers and sisters, the letter to the Galatians tells us that "when the designated time had come, God sent forth his Son born of a woman, born under the law, to deliver from the law those who were subjected to it, so that we might receive our status as adopted sons. The proof that you are sons is the fact that God has sent forth into our hearts the spirit of his Son which cries out 'Abba!' ('Father')" (Gal. 4:4-6). And it is to this woman, Mary the Mother of God and our Mother, ever obedient to the prompting of the Holy Spirit, that I confidently entrust your important work for renewal in and of the church. In the love of her Son, our Lord Jesus Christ, I willingly impart to you my Apostolic Blessing.

## AUDIENCE WITH THE BISHOPS
## OF SOUTHERN FRANCE 1982

*On December 16, 1982, Pope John Paul II received in audience
the ad limina visit of the bishops of southern France. He speaks
about spiritual renewal. In his discourse, the pope alludes to
what he said to the leaders of the renewal in May, 1981.*

That the pope would address the issue of the charismatic
renewal in a general address to the bishops of France on their ad
limina visit is a measure of the importance of the renewal in that
country. Here the pope is a model of the pastoral art: a joyful
openness to new initiatives of the Spirit, candid recognition of
problem areas in a broad popular movement in which every believer is a participant with something to give, care that in remov-
ing the rust from the surface the whole vessel not be broken, a
bold affirmation of support for the movement.

The pope notes that an intense spiritual quest is evident in
various groupings, which is manifested in a love of prayer. This
is to be looked upon as a grace to which one should be open.
Though the moment is opportune, one should not be surprised.
The church is a temple and the hearts of the believers a dwelling-
place in which the Spirit lives and prays. If this is what the
church is, it should not be a matter of surprise that new currents
make the church youthful. At no moment is the church without
the rejuvenating Spirit. Gratitude is the proper response to these
signs of newness of life. The Spirit elicits a love of contemplative
prayer which is the fountain at which evangelization is fed. The
pope rightly notes that the appearance of the renewal is accompanied by a vocation to evangelize.

The spiritual gifts manifested in the renewal are the common
heritage of the whole church, and should not be thought of as being sequestered in a particular movement. If the action of the
Spirit is evident in renewal groups it is in part due to the generosity with which Christians are giving themselves in various
ministries in the church. The work the Spirit is doing in these
groups is complementary to the episcopal vocation to evangelize.

The bishops will want to establish links with them, foster mutual love, and enter into dialogue and collaboration.

One of the reasons the renewal appeals to many is because it fulfills a real need in the church. The quality of the Christian life in the groups also draws many to them. Care must be taken as to the sources from which the renewal draws its nourishment. Those who would exalt sentiment to the detriment of doctrine would be confusing emotion with authentic religious experience. The demand for instant effects and the pursuit of the extraordinary can obscure the growth, slow and silent, of the word of God in the hearts of the faithful. Sudden conversions may have had long years of remote and proximate preparation in which the Spirit drew the person to cooperate with the grace of conversion received only after this long, hidden process.

Continuing discernment is necessary, a task which devolves upon the bishops. While being fully open to all the riches God has to offer, the bishops must interpret the meaning of the renewal. The discernment process in which the bishops are engaged is part of their responsibility for unity. Priests, who assure the ecclesial character of these groups, should gladly exercise their sacramental ministry for them.

The renewal is a sign that prayer has returned to its central place in the life of the church. Through Mary, the Mother of the church, the Holy Spirit is leading persons to find again the joy and the power of "their new baptism."

## THE INTENSE SPIRITUAL QUEST

. . . I am alluding to the intense spiritual quest which is observed in many Christians. I am referring concretely to spiritual renewal, but I am also thinking of the numerous prayer groups, various communities, workshops and meetings consecrated to prayer, retreats that are abundant in monasteries and other places of spiritual renewal, new places of pilgrimage. Also I refer to the rediscovery of prayer. If all this must be cared for and watched over, it is, first of all, a grace that comes in an opportune moment to sanctify the church. We are not to be surprised by it: "The Spirit dwells in the church and in the hearts of the faithful as in a temple (cf. 1 Cor. 3:16; 6:19) . . . He makes the church grow, perpetually renews her" (*Lumen Gentium,* 4). The Spirit continues acting in the church through these spiritual currents, for which we are grateful. In these currents it becomes evident that the joy of prayer is reborn: personal and community prayer, a prayer which is praise and intercession and wants to be a form of contemplation and a fountain of evangelization. Indeed, the Spirit acts in all these manifestations provided that they are built upon the word of God, are nourished by the sacraments and are rooted in the church.

Moreover, no one can appropriate to oneself exclusively a spiritual inheritance which belongs to the entire church. If the action of the Spirit becomes obvious in the way these groups and even communities of the faithful spring up, to him is due also the generosity with which an increasing number of Christians, for love of the Lord and in a spirit of faith and prayer, are dedicating themselves to doing the work of the church in the various ministries in the liturgy, catechesis, in Christian movements and charitable works in the parish and the diocese, and even more far-reaching than that. "It is important to be aware of your complementarity and to establish bonds . . . , not only mutual esteem and dialogue, but a certain harmony as well and even real collaboration," as I said to the laity in Paris (May 31, 1980, section 2).

*Renewal Appeals Because the Need for Renewal Is Recognized*
The existence of spiritual renewal appeals to the communities of believers, above all, because the need is there, and because of the quality of the Christian resurgence. And, in turn, the church, of which they form a part, appeals to those who more energetically promote this renewal. It would not be right that currents, whose vitality surprises us, should be mixed in waters flowing from other fountains. For example, a certain distrust of doctrine would run the risk of leaving too much room for sentiment. If that happens there would be a confusion of emotion and spiritual experience, something which would be prejudicial. In the same way, the desire for immediate efficacy and the

desire for certain kinds of prodigies or extraordinary things can lead to forgetting the slow and silent maturing of the word of God in the heart of the believer. If it appears that the Holy Spirit bursts suddenly into the life of a man or a woman, which results in a conversion, one must not omit taking into account either the proximate or remote preparations which the Spirit uses in general, with which it is a duty to cooperate. Faith relies on time [=a colloquial expression meaning that patience in time will eventually disclose the true nature of the experience].

### Role of Bishops and Priests
In a word, all these things depend on the discernment of spirits. One is to remember the golden rule formulated by the apostle Saint Paul: "To each person the manifestation of the Spirit is given for the common good" (1 Cor. 12:7). Therefore, it is now up to you [the bishops], first of all, to see how best to interpret the meaning which must be given to spiritual renewal, and how to adapt it, as I myself said: "a model of growth and development fully open to all the riches of the love of God in his church" (May 7, 1981, section 3). In your turn, you who are responsible for unity, each one in his place, has to do the work of discernment. It devolves upon the priests, above all, to guarantee the ecclesial character of every group of the faithful. Let them pay great attention to this aspect of their responsibility. Let them practice gladly the sacramental ministry in the groups, communities and gatherings who ask for it, and let them do it in agreement with you . . . . Your other role is to encourage the renewal. Religious men and women who join in the spiritual renewal are not to loosen the bonds with their religious charism, or become slack in the obedience due to their legitimate superiors.

We are to take care to give words the meaning they have in the language of the church. The vocabulary of the religious life does not always correspond with these new forms of groupings that are still looking for their canonical identity. After affirming these issues, let us rejoice in stating that prayer is again coming back to take its central

place in the church. Without recourse to the Holy Spirit—
who is really the soul of the church—how could this
church unfold its dynamism and apostolic wisdom? That
does not diminish in any way the theological task of which
I have spoken. Both go hand in hand . . . . And through
Mary, Mother of the church, the Holy Spirit leads Christians to find again the joy and dynamism of the grace of
their new baptism.

Document 14

## FIFTH INTERNATIONAL LEADERS' CONFERENCE 1984

*On the occasion of the Fifth International Leaders' Conference,
Pope John Paul II addressed the participants on April 30, 1984.*

*The pope reminds the conference of leaders that they are called
to share in the church's vocation to evangelize in their local
churches. The renewal has rediscovered the importance of the
sacraments, which are the full realization of the word of God.
The pope thus joins the word of God to the sacramental life of the
church.*

*The quest for God must be seen as a personal encounter with
the Lord in the church, which through the Holy Spirit is the
sacrament of salvation. In referring to the "personal moment" in
faith the pope recognizes an emphasis often found in the renewal
as an antidote to a purely objective, extrinsic faith, but that moment of encounter has a specific ecclesial, sacramental character.*

*The return to the sacramental sources makes it possible to have
an enduring personal encounter in response to the invitation,
"Remain in my love." The power to witness and evangelize, a
theme which frequently surfaces in the renewal, flows from Baptism and Confirmation ministered in the local churches. The union of the personal and the ecclesial aspects makes the meeting at
the center of the church, Rome, important for the whole charismatic renewal.*

*In celebrating Pentecost we find Mary in the midst of the apostles. She is the one who accepted the Holy Spirit's greatest gift: the life of Jesus. Mary, who is the Mother of the church, should be the mother and model of the renewal in the church.*

## CRY OUT, "OPEN THE DOORS"

Dear Brothers and Sisters: With all my heart I welcome you to Rome in the joy of the Risen Christ. Your meeting in Rome, at the center of the church, comes at a time when she is giving thanks to the Father of our Lord Jesus Christ for the sacrifice of his Son and for the action of the Holy Spirit, which fill her with new life.

As I said in my Easter message, the Holy Door of the Jubilee Year of the Redemption has now been closed, but we must remember that at Easter the door of Christ's tomb was opened once and for all. He who is the Resurrection and the Life knows nothing of closed doors which do not open for him. For this reason I ask you, and all the members of the charismatic renewal, to continue to cry aloud to the world with me: "Open the doors to the Redeemer."

The church's mission is to proclaim Christ to the world. You share effectively in this mission insofar as your groups and communities are rooted in the local churches, in your dioceses and parishes.

The Jubilee Year of the Redemption has brought us back to the source, to "the heart of the church," the only source that can nourish our Christian life. It has enabled the People of God throughout the world to rediscover the importance of the sacraments, notably the sacraments of Reconciliation and Eucharist. Because they are the full enactment of the word of God, they are the most precious gifts that he has given to us in his Son, our Lord Jesus Christ.

*The Turn to the Sacraments and Other Sources*

I am particularly pleased that you are concentrating on the sacraments in your reflections. This is of the greatest significance. All your spiritual efforts must be directed to a personal encounter of each individual with the Lord in the community of the church, which, through the power of the Holy Spirit, is herself the great sacrament of salvation.

Real openness to the Holy Spirit as he vivifies and guides the church helps you to live in union with the Lord Jesus. It is your strength and your special treasure, and you are striving to exercise it in different ways. But this gift from God is also a fragile treasure and one of which you must take special care. It is for this reason that your international meeting at the center of the church, at a time so strongly marked by the jubilee of the redemption, can be of decisive importance for the whole Catholic charismatic renewal.

I would interpret your presence here, and your choice of themes for your discussions, as a decision to return to the sources: to center your whole lives on the encounter with the Redeemer in his sacraments. It is precisely the openness of the human heart to the sacramental grace that God offers you in the church (which) enables you to meet Christ in a real and lasting way, to respond to his loving command: "Remain in my love" (Jn. 15:9).

I mentioned that you are rooted in your local churches. The church herself as a sacramental reality communicates the grace of the sacraments through the ministry of priests in the local churches. At the sacramental heart of the church and at the sacramental heart of your local churches your life as baptized and confirmed Christians can be ceaselessly renewed—that life which in the power of the Spirit makes you witnesses to Christ the Redeemer.

Soon we shall celebrate Pentecost. In the midst of the apostles there is Mary, the one who accepted the Holy Spirit's greatest gift: the life of Jesus. May she who thus became the Mother of the Church be in a special way your Mother and the model of the renewal in the church. Let us entrust to her our lives, our commitment and our desire to grow in the love of Jesus Christ and in fidelity to his holy church.

## CHARISMATIC YOUTH CONFERENCE 1985

*In 1985 the International Youth Year was celebrated. The youth involved in the renewal held a conference in Rome, and on this occasion were invited to a Eucharist in the Clementine Room of the Vatican, presided over by the pope. Before beginning the celebration the pope spoke briefly.*

Dear Brothers and Sisters, on the occasion of the International Youth Conference held at *Domus Pacis* in Rome, and organized by the International Catholic Charismatic Renewal Office, you have expressed the wish to pray with the pope. I am happy to greet you this morning as you join me in this celebration of the Eucharist. In this International Youth Year I am especially pleased to welcome you, who are youth leaders in the church. You are well aware that young people enjoy a special place in my heart. Therefore I have a great desire to offer encouragement and support to leaders of youth like yourself. You can be sure that I pray for you often and it is a joy to be with you today.

The liturgy is the focal point of all the activities of the church. United with Christ and with one another, we place ourselves before our heavenly Father and offer him our hymn of thanksgiving and praise. We also bring to him our desires and needs. At this Mass, in which we are all celebrating the feast of St. Ignatius of Antioch, we pray for all young people throughout the world and in particular for those in the church. We ask God, our Father, to draw them ever closer to himself and to the heart of his only Son, our Lord, Jesus Christ. Now to prepare ourselves to celebrate these sacred mysteries. . . .

## THE ENCYCLICAL
## *THE LORD AND GIVER OF LIFE* 1986

*From the encyclical* The Lord and Giver of Life *(Dominum et Vivificantem), published May 18, 1986, section 65 is extracted here. In an audience with the directors of the International Catholic Charismatic Renewal Office, the pope said: "This encyclical is for you!"*

*In this section of the encyclical the pope expounds the relation of the Spirit to prayer. Wherever there is prayer, there also is the Spirit. The Holy Spirit is present both in favorable situations and in hostile environments. For all voiceless persons, prayer is a voice. In prayer are opened up those great depths which only God can fill.*

*When we have no prayer, when we have nothing to say, but only the desire to pray, the Spirit within prays with a divine force. The Spirit knows the human heart and the heart of God. The Spirit prays within according to the mind of God.*

*More than once the pope has spoken of the rediscovery of prayer. Various movements and groups have restored primacy to the life of prayer, which has contributed to a revival of prayer generally among the faithful. A better understanding of the Holy Spirit and an openness to the divine promptings of the Spirit bring about great longing for holiness.*

*Technology threatens our achievements, threatens the whole of human life. This has prompted individuals and groups to discover prayer. To find prayer is to find our weakness. In that moment in which we come to face our infirmity in prayer, we rediscover the Spirit.*

## THE SPIRIT BREATHES PRAYER
The breath of the divine life, the Holy Spirit, in its simplest and most common manner, expresses itself and makes itself felt in prayer. It is a beautiful and salutary thought that, wherever people are praying in the world, there the Holy Spirit is, the living breath of prayer. It is a beautiful

and salutary thought to recognize that, if prayer is offered throughout the world, in the past, in the present and in the future, equally widespread is the presence and action of the Holy Spirit, who "breathes" prayer in the heart of man in all the endless range of the most varied situations and conditions, sometimes favorable and sometimes unfavorable to the spiritual and religious life.

Many times, through the influence of the Spirit, prayer rises from the human heart in spite of prohibitions and persecutions and even official proclamations regarding the nonreligious or even atheistic character of public life. Prayer always remains the voice of all those who apparently have no voice—and in this voice there always echoes that "loud cry" attributed to Christ by the letter to the Hebrews (Heb. 5:7).

Prayer is also the revelation of that abyss which is the heart of man: a depth which comes from God and which only God can fill, precisely with the Holy Spirit. We read in Luke: "If you then, who are evil, know how to give good gifts to your children, how much more will the heavenly Father give the Holy Spirit to those who ask him!" (Lk. 11:13).

*The Spirit Gives and Guides Prayer*

The Holy Spirit is the gift that comes into man's heart together with prayer. In prayer he manifests himself first of all and above all as the gift that "helps us in our weakness." This is the magnificent thought developed by Saint Paul in the letter to the Romans, when he writes: "For we do not know how to pray as we ought, but the Spirit himself intercedes for us with sighs too deep for words" (Rm. 8:26).

Therefore, the Holy Spirit not only enables us to pray, but guides us "from within" in prayer: he is present in our prayer and gives it a divine dimension (cf. Origen, *On Prayer* 2; PG 11:419-423). Thus "he who searches the hearts of men knows what is the mind of the Spirit, because the Spirit intercedes for the saints according to the will of God" (Rm. 8:27). Prayer through the power of the Holy

Spirit becomes the ever more mature expression of the new man, who by means of this prayer participates in the divine life.

Our difficult age has a special need of prayer. In the course of history—both in the past and in the present—many men and women have borne witness to the importance of prayer by consecrating themselves to the praise of God and to the life of prayer, especially in monasteries and convents; so too recent years have been seeing a growth in the number of people who, in ever more widespread movements and groups, are giving first place to prayer and seeking in prayer a renewal of their spiritual life. This is a significant and comforting sign, for from this experience there is coming a real contribution to the revival of prayer among the faithful, who have been helped to gain a clearer idea of the Holy Spirit as he who inspires in hearts a profound yearning for holiness.

### Technology Reveals the Void Which the Spirit Fills

In many individuals and many communities there is a growing awareness that, even with all the rapid progress of technological and scientific civilization, and despite the real conquests and goals attained, man is threatened, humanity is threatened. In the face of this danger, and indeed already experiencing the frightful reality of man's spiritual decadence, individuals and whole communities, guided as it were by an inner sense of faith, are seeking the strength to raise man up again, to save him from himself, from his own errors and mistakes that often make harmful his very conquests. Thus they are discovering prayer, in which the "Spirit who helps us in our weakness" manifests himself.

In this way the times in which we are living are bringing the Holy Spirit closer to the many who are turning to prayer. I trust that all will find in the teaching of this encyclical nourishment for their interior life, and that they will succeed in strengthening, under the action of the Spirit, their commitment to prayer in harmony with the church and her magisterium.

## AUDIENCE WITH THE ITALIAN
## CHARISMATIC RENEWAL 1986

*On November 15, 1986, about 15,000 participants in the charis-*
*matic renewal of Italy were received by the pope in St. Peter's*
*Basilica.*

*The pope quotes the section of the encyclical* The Lord and
Giver of Life *to which he had also alluded in his address to the*
*directors of* ICCRO *on May 18, 1986. More specifically he refers to*
*the rediscovery of prayer. To that theme he now adds conversion.*
*Authentic renewal has certain characteristics: integrality, spe-*
*cificity and an ecclesial sense.*

*Life in the Spirit, lived to a heroic degree, does not find sup-*
*port in the "in" life-style. The current fashion in life-style makes*
*it difficult to distinguish true values from their imitation. Life in*
*the Spirit means being ruled by "the reasons of the Spirit" in our*
*quest for God, and also in the way we relate to one another. To*
*be formed by the gospel is to return to the renunciation and the*
*promises implicit in our Baptism, which are summed up in the*
*love of God and neighbor. The way of love excels even the most*
*special charisms.*

*The best way to live according to the Spirit is to be ruled by*
*the Beatitudes proclaimed by Jesus. To walk in the Spirit is to*
*come under the law of the Spirit which establishes us in a new*
*manner of life. The new law is not an external code, but is rather*
*the very presence of the Spirit written in the heart.*

*The church itself comes under this interior law. If the church*
*has strength and vigor it is because the law within is the Spirit,*
*the source of the church's mission.*

*Those who cleave to the church, share the church's faith, obey*
*the laws of the church, and insert themselves into the mission*
*which is properly that of the church — those who do these things*
*lay hold of God's plan, and draw strength from the principle of*
*the church's life, the Spirit, the soul of the church.*

*If there is a churchlike communion, it is to be found here: a*
*communion of faith, a communion with the bishops and priests, a*

*communion with Peter, and as the ultimate "place" of all and any*
*communion, a communion in the Holy Spirit.*

## THE REASONS OF THE SPIRIT

It gives me great joy to find myself with you, beloved
brothers and sisters of the "Renewal in the Spirit," since I
have already manifested my esteem to you, at the audience of November 23, 1980, and recalled the teachings of
the church about the action of the Holy Spirit in souls and
in Christian communities.

Your presence in this basilica, where you have shared in
the celebration of Holy Mass, is for me reason to rejoice,
not only for your witness of sincere faith, but also because
you offer me the opportunity of conversing with you about
some aspects of the ideals and program of your movement, six months after the encyclical on the Holy Spirit,
*The Lord and Giver of Life*, published on the occasion of the
past Solemnity of Pentecost.

Certainly, you have not forgotten the page on which,
speaking of prayer as a need in our difficult epoch, I pointed out the fact that the testimony to the importance of
prayer, given in the course of history by men and women
dedicated to the praise of God and to the life of prayer,
above all, in monasteries, is today adding an increasing
number of faithful, who, as I wrote in the encyclical—"in
ever more widespread movements and groups, (persons)
are giving first place to prayer and seeking in prayer a
renewal of their spiritual life. This is a significant and comforting sign, for from this experience there is coming a real
contribution to the revival of prayer among the faithful,
who have been helped to gain a clearer idea of the Holy
Spirit as he who inspires in hearts a profound yearning for
holiness" (section 65).

In this context must be placed every project of renewal
which wants to accomplish in our time what Saint Paul
recommended long ago to the Christians at Ephesus,
when, calling them to "the truth that is in Jesus," he
reminded them of their duty "to put off your old nature
which belongs to your former manner of life, and is cor-

rupt through deceitful lusts." He continued: "Be renewed in the spirit of your minds, and put on the new nature, created after the likeness of God in true righteousness and holiness" (Eph. 4:21-24; cf. 2:15; Rm. 13:14; Col. 3:5, 9-10). The truth of Christ must be, then, the truth of man, the truth of life!

### The Truth That Is in Jesus

In the Pauline text appear two fundamental notes of authentic renewal: "The truth of Jesus," which is "true holiness," and the "inner depth" ("Be renewed in your spirit"). In other passages of his letters, the apostle underlines other characteristics of charismatic renewal, among them integrality, specificity and the ecclesial. In fact, he enumerates the vices that are to be avoided, the virtues that must be practiced, and the behavior that is to be observed in interpersonal relations, family ties, social and ecclesiastical matters, in order to be truly "the new man," the "new creation" (cf. 2 Cor. 5:17; Gal. 3:27; Rm. 13:14) in the communion of the Body of Christ (cf. Eph. 4:4; 1 Cor. 12: 13). Gathering together, as in one sole exhortation, all the others, he says: "Do not grieve the Holy Spirit of God, in whom you were sealed for the day of redemption" (Eph. 4:30). The light of this teaching of the apostle, which is in perfect tune with the gospel of Jesus, helps you understand what renewal can mean, to which you are so committed and which the church for her part encourages you to pursue, supporting you and directing you according to the mission received from the same Jesus.

### Live According to the Spirit

First of all, it treats of a conversion and of a growth, always new in the "life of the Spirit," struggling against the temptations to theoretical and practical materialism. Today this materialism carries on to the ultimate consequences its resistance to the "promptings of the Spirit," not excluding opposition to God or, at least, disinterest and indifference. In fact, we find ourselves in a cultural and social context where the flowering of prayer and virtue – practiced even in our days by numerous faithful with acts of great moral value, often to the point of heroism – finds no help in the so-called current fashionable life-style. The same mentality is itself contaminated by materialism to such a degree that with respect to conscience it becomes more and more difficult to judge true values, to distinguish them from pseudovalues. In certain aspects, the situation comes near to what Saint Paul had to face when writing to the Christians of Galatia. He insisted: "I tell you, therefore, walk in the Spirit and do not yield to the cravings of the flesh" (Gal. 5:16), nor give in to the "works of the flesh" (Gal. 5:19-21), nor, finally, to "live according to the flesh" (Rom. 8:5f).

The first dimension of renewal consists, therefore, in this: "to live according to the Spirit," in this continual growing in the Spirit, resisting the gratifications of the "flesh," opening oneself to the strong, sweet attraction of God. This inner renewal, this healing of the very roots of life and this formation of a mentality dominated by the "promptings of the Spirit" is your vocation as Christians, your vocation as men and women, youths and adults of our time who want to give witness, who want that model to flourish in the world of today, the model of spirituality and even of courtesy, which we see illumined in the norms of life given by Saint Paul.

The second dimension of the "renewal" is deduced from the urgent need, which you feel so intimately, to reaffirm the value of the principles and criteria of the gospel, as laws of the spiritual life and the leaven of social life. For a time, the said principles were manifested even in the "eternal norms" taught by the saints and traditionally transmitted from generation to generation in the Christian world. Today these norms are unknown and sometimes rejected and scorned, even by many Christians who have forgotten the "renunciations" and the "promises" of Baptism. To these it is necessary to return, because in them are expressed those gospel values which can be summed up in the law of the love of God and of neighbor (cf. Jn. 13:34). It is a question of the "better way" which Saint Paul, always in tune with Jesus, shows to the Corinthians as far more excellent and necessary than even the most select charismatic gifts (1 Cor. 12:28-30; 13:1f): again and always, charity. It is a question of an ethical and ascetical itinerary through which can be realized the perfection of the Christian life with the acceptance and the following of the "beatitudes" proclaimed by Jesus (cf. Mt. 5:3f).

Behold, beloved sons and daughters, a great program of renewal: the message of the beatitudes which makes us perform the "works of the Spirit" and "live according to the Spirit," even in the present-day social context. Christians today are called to make this program effective.

### The New Law

We take this path of charity and of the beatitudes under the impulse and guidance of the Holy Spirit. He has been sent to the church and to the world in order to make real the fullness of the victory won by Christ over sin, with the purification of consciences, the liberation of men from the "works" and "desires of the flesh," the infusion into hearts of "the desires according to the Spirit," the strengthening of the inner man, the renewal and continual growth of personal and social life until reaching the "status of that perfect Man who is Christ come to full stature" (Eph. 4:13) on earth and in heaven.

Of all this, I have spoken in the second and in the third part of the encyclical *The Lord and Giver of Life*, in which you will be able to find the third dimension of the renewal explained. This consists in what Saint Paul calls "the law of the Spirit who gives life in Christ Jesus." This law has freed us from the "law of sin and of death" (Rm. 8:2), restoring in man redeemed a new system of life, that of the Spirit or, rather, of the same Holy Spirit who is present and acts in the spirit of man (cf. 1:9; 3:27; 5:5; 8:9; 6:11). It treats of the "new law" which according to Saint Augustine "is written in the hearts of the faithful" (*On the Spirit and the Letter*, c. 24) and "is identified with the presence of the Holy Spirit" (ibid., c. 21).

### The Primacy of the Grace of the Spirit

Saint Thomas uses this idea to give primacy to "the grace of the Holy Spirit" as the essential content and living force of Christianity. Everything that is visible, organized, written and preached in the church has been instituted and ordered to the service of grace (*"sicut dispositiva ad gratiam Spiritus Sancti et ad usum huius gratiae pertinentia"*: I-II, q. 106, a. 1). The church thus appears in all the vigor of its divine constitution, but also in its essential function as ordered to grace, as bride and collaborator of the Holy Spirit in invoking and in preparing the ever new coming of the Lord Jesus (cf. Rev. 22:20), as I wrote at the end of the encyclical on Pentecost (cf. *The Lord and Giver of Life*, sections 65-66).

To adhere to the church, to remain united to her, to share her faith, to obey her laws, to collaborate in her mission—even within the sphere of the dioceses and parishes in which the family of believers in Christ are distributed—is the sure road to arrive at the heart of the economy of grace and to drink at the fountain of the Holy Spirit the energies capable of fulfilling the renewal of persons and of communities.

### Communion with Peter

Your presence, beloved brothers and sisters, near to the successor of Peter, visible head of the universal church, and the repeated reaffirmations of sincere and active communion with him and with the bishops of your local churches, signifies that you have understood well what the gospel teaches, what the Holy Spirit, present in hearts, inspires as the central principle of the "new law," as the fundamental rule of action and of ecclesial prayer, as the sure secret of all renewal and of all progress: to be at the service of the reign of Christ in accord with the indications of the Spirit in the communion of faith, of thought and of discipline with the pastors of the Church.

I express my good wishes for your perseverance and progress along this road, while, upon you and on your aspirations for good, on your plans and work, I invoke the divine benediction, of which let my blessing be a pledge.

## AUDIENCE WITH THE BISHOPS OF NORTHERN FRANCE 1987

*On January 22, 1987, a group of bishops from the region of northern France, who were fulfilling their ad limina visit, were addressed by the pope on a number of topics, among them the charismatic renewal.*

*Through the charismatic renewal prayer groups have spontaneously sprung up. Such groups can foster the classical forms of prayer as well as the more exuberant. Some pastors have shown reserve and, indeed, pastoral oversight is necessary so that the force and generosity found in these groups not extinguish or preempt other parish initiatives. Still, after one has gone through a discernment process one can speak of the renewal as a grace for the church. This is seen in its delight in prayer, in praise, in intercession. All of this becomes a new source for evangelization.*

## A GRACE FOR THE CHURCH

. . . Nowadays, there exists another possibility: that of prayer groups which have multiplied in the Catholic Church as in other church communities, and this spontaneously, in an unexpected manner. Prayer can be developed here in a classic way. It can also seek the support of the more exuberant manifestations. Some pastors have received this movement with restraint. And, in fact, it is necessary to keep watch always so that an authentic doctrine inspires this type of prayer, and the ecclesial character of the sacramental ministers may be well respected, and that the tasks of charity and justice are not abandoned. On the other hand, the dynamism and generosity of these groups should not impede other initiatives animating the life of parish communities. However, with all necessary discernment, it is possible to speak of a grace directed to sanctify the church, to renew in her the taste for prayer, to rediscover, with the Holy Spirit, the sense of gratuitousness, of joyful praise, of confidence in intercession, and to be converted into a new fountain of evangelization (cf. Discourse to the Bishops of Southern France, December 16, 1982).

## Document 19

### SIXTH INTERNATIONAL LEADERS' CONFERENCE 1987

*From May 11 to 16, 1987, the Sixth International Leaders' Conference met in Rome to reflect on the theme "Good News for the Poor." On May 15 the pope welcomed the 1,000 leaders present at the conference.*

*When Jesus began his public ministry he declared, "The Spirit of the Lord is upon me." With these words Jesus indicates two things about his ministry: it is carried out in the power of the Spirit, and in a special way it is directed to the poor. These two qualities drew the crowds to Jesus in those days. Today they draw us again.*

*"The Spirit of the Lord is upon me" qualifies Jesus' entry into public ministry. From this accent on Jesus and the emphasis on the Spirit the pope wishes to say that the two belong together, and together they constitute the identity of the church, the mission of the church, and the identity of the individual Christian. The charismatic renewal, then, is not to be associated with an exaggerated, one-sided doctrine of the Spirit. Jesus and the Spirit are kept in tension, in a relationship of mutuality and reciprocity. Jesus and the Spirit are in movement, at the Father's initiative, toward the church and the world. They are also in movement, at the Father's initiative, back to the absolute start, the Father.*

*"The Spirit of the Lord is upon me," because the reality here announced to belong to the identity of Jesus also describes the character of the church since the day of Pentecost, when the Spirit was sent to sanctify and give access back to the origin of all life, the Father.*

*The charismatic renewal is a sign of the powerful presence of the Spirit at work in the church. The entrance of the Spirit is not to be dated from the rise of the charismatic renewal. In every age the Spirit and the charisms were present in the church, but the renewal itself is a bold statement of what "the Spirit is saying to the churches" at the end of the second thousand years. Because of the power of the Spirit in the renewal, it is all the more necessary that the many levels of communion be deepened: communion in the sacraments, in doctrine, with the bishops and pastors, in discipline.*

*"The Spirit of the Lord is upon me" belongs also to one's personal identity as a Christian. As it was for Jesus, so it is for us a personal vocation to bring relief to the poor and to proclaim to them the Good News.*

*Mary, overshadowed by the Spirit, is a model for every believer. The experience of many Christians today is not altogether unlike Mary's experience of the Spirit. The overshadowing Spirit dwelling within the Christian is addressed as "Lord," the one who gives life. Because the Spirit brings the riches and glory of God, the Christian confronts the spiritual deprivation in human life and the need for a savior. Seeing that all, poor and rich, come with empty hands to be filled with the bread of the Word, and the bread of the Body, one is forced to realize one's solidarity with the poor. The Good News for the poor can only be the Good News for us. Mary has her part in that oneness with the poor because in the Magnificat she proclaims the coming of the messiah of the poor. In that canticle Mary makes clear how intimately the God who saves prefers the poor. God exalts the lowly, raises them up, gives them the first places usually reserved for the wealthy and the powerful.*

In this address the pope uses the vocabulary often found in liberation theology, namely, the preferential option for the poor. Pope John Paul II confronts the renewal's call to interiority and adoration with the demand of the gospel that the poor be served.

*One does not choose between the prayer of praise and feeding the hungry; one chooses both. The poor who are in want of food and justice, and have no voice in their own future, are the object of God's special choice and favor. If the elect are to be identified with any group, says Mary in the Magnificat, it is with the lowly who are without power. The gospel Mary announces is the same gospel Jesus proclaims.*

## THE SPIRIT IDENTIFIES JESUS

Dear Brothers and Sisters: In the peace and joy of the Holy Spirit I welcome all of you who have come to Rome for the Sixth International Leaders' Conference of the Catholic charismatic renewal. I am very happy to meet you today and, as I begin, I wish to assure you that your love for Christ and your openness to the Spirit of Truth are a most valuable witness in the church's mission in the world.

You are prayerfully considering, during these days, the words of the prophet Isaiah which Jesus made his own at the very beginning of his public ministry: "The Spirit of the Lord is upon me, because he has anointed me to preach good news to the poor" (Lk. 4:18).

These words, when read by Jesus in the synagogue at Nazareth, had a profound effect on those listening. As he finished the reading, he rolled up the scroll and sat down, and "the eyes of all in the synagogue were fixed on him" (Lk. 4:20). Even in our own time, these prophetic words strike to the heart. They draw us upward in faith to the person of Christ and deepen our desire "to fix our eyes on him," the redeemer of the world, the perfect fulfillment of all prophecy. They stir up our longing to enter ever more completely into the mystery of Christ: to know him better and to love him with greater fidelity.

### The Spirit Identifies the Church

"The Spirit of the Lord is upon me." While Jesus applied these words to himself that day in Nazareth, they could likewise be applied at Pentecost and thereafter to the Body of Christ, the church. "When the work which the Father had given to the Son to do on earth (cf. Jn. 17:4) was accomplished, the Holy Spirit was sent on the day of Pentecost in order that he might forever sanctify the church, and thus all believers would have access to the Father through Christ in the one Spirit" (*Lumen Gentium*, 4). As a result, the history of the church is at the same time the history of 2,000 years of the action of the Holy Spirit, "the Lord, the Giver of Life," who renews God's people in grace and freedom, and is "the Spirit of Truth," bringing holiness and joy to people of every race and tongue and nation.

### Twentieth Anniversary of the Renewal

This year marks the 20th anniversary of the charismatic renewal in the Catholic Church. The vigor and fruitfulness of the renewal certainly attest to the powerful presence of the Holy Spirit at work in the church in these years after the Second Vatican Council. Of course, the Spirit has guided the church in every age, producing a great variety of gifts among the faithful. Because of the Spirit, the church preserves a continual youthful vitality, and the charismatic renewal is an eloquent manifestation of this vitality today, a bold statement of what "the Spirit is saying to the churches" (Rev. 2:7) as we approach the close of the second millennium.

For this reason, it is essential that you seek always to deepen your communion with the whole church: with her doctrine and discipline, with her sacramental life, with the entire People of God.

In this same regard I have asked Bishop Paul Cordes to assist as episcopal adviser to the International Catholic Charismatic Renewal Office. I am sure that he will help you in fostering a dynamism that is always well-balanced and in strengthening your bonds of fidelity to the Apostolic See.

### The Spirit Identifies the Christian

"The Spirit of the Lord is upon me." In addition to the meaning of these words for Jesus and for the church throughout the world, they also remind us of our own personal identities as men and women who have been baptized into Christ. For us, the Spirit of the Lord is upon us, each one of us, who have been born anew in the saving waters of Baptism. The Spirit prompts us to go forth in faith "to preach good news to the poor": the poor in material things, the poor in spiritual gifts, the poor in mind and body. The Holy Spirit gives us the courage and strength to go out to all who, in a particular way, are the "little ones" of the world. All of us respond in a unique manner, according to our own special talents and gifts, but we shall be able to make a generous and authentic response only if we are firmly grounded in a regular habit of prayer.

Accordingly, I recommend that you meditate on these words of Isaiah frequently, pondering the great mystery of how the Spirit of God overshadows your life in a manner not altogether dissimilar to the experience of Mary. As the truth penetrates your heart and soul, it fills your whole being with gratitude and praise and a sense of awe at God's great love.

### The Spirit Identifies Prayer and Ministry

"The Spirit of the Lord is upon me." These words stand at the foundation of our prayer, our service to others, our life of faith. They direct us toward the invisible God who dwells within us as in a temple, to the one whom we profess in the Creed to be "the Lord, the Giver of Life," the one who "has spoken through the prophets." In prayerful reflection on these words, we meet and adore the Holy Spirit.

In prayer, too, we come to see the stark reality of our own poverty, the absolute need we have for a Savior. We discover to a more profound degree the many ways in which we ourselves are poor and needy, and thus we begin to feel an increasing solidarity with all the poor. In the end, we realize more fully than ever before that the Good News for the poor is Good News for ourselves as well.

### Mary and the Preferential Option for the Poor

Dear Friends in Christ, you have come to Rome in the month of May, Our Lady's month. You come just prior to

64

the Feast of Pentecost and the beginning of the Marian Year. In considering the theme, "Good News to the Poor," you are considering a theme dear to the Mother of our redeemer. As I state in my recent encyclical on the Blessed Virgin Mary in the life of the church, "Mary truly proclaims the coming of 'the Messiah of the poor' " (cf. Is. 11:4; 61:1). Drawing from Mary's heart, from the depth of her faith expressed in the words of the Magnificat, the church renews ever more effectively in herself the awareness that the truth about the God who saves, the truth about the God who is the source of every gift, cannot be separated from the manifestation of his preferential love for the poor and humble, that love which, celebrated in the Magnificat, is later expressed in the words and works of Jesus" (*The Mother of the Redeemer* (*Redemptoris Mater*), 37).

May you be inspired by the heroic example of love given by the Virgin Mother of our redeemer, and may you entrust yourselves with confidence to her intercession and maternal care. In the love of her Son, our Savior Christ the Lord, I impart to all of you my Apostolic Blessing.

# NOTES

1. New York: Crossroads, 1987. 2. Doc. 5. 3. Ibid. 4. Doc. 13. 5. Doc. 4 and 5. 6. Doc. 19. 7. Ibid. 8. Doc. 5. This is a reference to *Dogmatic Constitution on the Church*, 12. 9. Doc. 4. 10. Doc. 13. 11. Ibid. 12. Doc. 5. 13. Doc. 11. 14. Doc. 13. 15. Doc. 11. 16. Doc. 19. 17. Doc. 5. 18. Ibid. 19. Ibid. 20. Doc. 6. 21. Doc. 10. 22. Doc. 12. 23. Doc. 13. 24. Doc. 12. 25. Ibid. 26. Doc. 9. 27. Doc. 19.

28. A quite acceptable nonsacramental view has been proposed by Francis Sullivan, " 'Baptism in the Holy Spirit': A Catholic Interpretation of the Pentecostal Experience," *Gregorianum* (1974), pp. 49-68; idem., "Baptism in the Spirit," *Charism and Charismatic Renewal* (Ann Arbor: Servant, 1982), pp. 59-75. This appears to have its foundation in the early days of the church, and possibly back in biblical times.

29. Aidan Kavanaugh, *The Shape of Baptism: The Rite of Christian Initiation* (New York: Pueblo, 1974), p. 26.

30. Nils Dahl, "The Origin of Baptism," *Interpretationes ad Vetus Testamentum pertinentes Sigmundo Mowinckel* (Oslo: Forlaget Land og Kirke, 1955), p. 46.

31. *The Church with a Human Face* (New York: Crossroads, 1987), p. 37.

32. Ibid., 34, 35, 122, 123.

33. Ibid., 37, 73, 83, 122.

34. Ibid., 36.

35. Ibid., 120.

36. *Dialogue with Trypho* 29:1.

37. *On the Trinity* 2:12.

38. *On Baptism* 8. Hereafter cited as OB.

39. Ibid., 20.

40. See the introduction of André Tuilier to *Sources Chré-tiennes* 248:52, 53.

41. *Dialogue with Trypho* 82.

42. *Against Heresies* 5,6,1. See also 1,13,4; 4, 26,5.

43. Ibid., 3,11,9.

44. *Patrology* (Westminster: Christian Classics, 1986) II, 280. This is also the judgment of Ernest Evans in his introduction to *Tertullian's Homily on Baptism* (London: SPCK, 1964), p. xi.

45. For a technical article reviewing the Tertullian evidence in more detail see Kilian McDonnell, "Communion Ecclesiology, Tertullian, and the Baptism in the Holy Spirit," *Theological Studies* 49 (1988).

46. Ibid., 3,363. I am indebted to Father Raniero Cantalamessa, O.F.M. Cap., for calling my attention to Cyril's text.

47. "For what fellowship have you with men without hope, you, who are about to be baptized in the Holy Spirit," *Catechetical Lectures* 16:6. Hereafter cited as *CL*. "If you pretend (to have faith, whereas you have none) he (the bishop) will indeed baptize you, but the Spirit will not baptize you." *CL* 17:36.

48. *CL* 16:2, 22.     49. *CL* 16:22.     50. *CL* 16:12.     51. *CL* 16:12, 19, 22.     52. *CL* 18:23.     53. *CL* 17:37.     54. *CL* 17:18.     55. *CL* 17:14, 15, 18; PG 33:985, 988, 989.     56. *CL* 18:32.     57. *Mystagogical Catechesis* 3:2.     58. Ibid., 3:2. 59. Ibid.     60. Poitiers is located about 180 miles southwest of Paris, France.     61. *Tract on the Psalms*, 64:14. 62. Ibid.     63. Ibid., 64:15.     64. Ibid., 16:14.     65. Ibid., 64:12, 14.     66. Ibid., 64:14.     67. Ibid., 64:6, 14.

68. This sacramental view of the baptism in the Hcly Spirit does not suggest that reality of the baptism is found only in the sacramental churches. God is not imprisoned in his own plan of salvation.

69. "Statement of the Theological Basis of the Catholic Charismatic Renewal," *Presence, Power, Praise: Documents on the Charismatic Renewal* (3 vols.; Collegeville: Liturgical Press: 1980) III, 1-11.